EXPORT
COMPLIANCE
A Practical Guide to Licensing and Controls

By
Nancy Wood-Kouassi

BOSKAGE COMMERCE PUBLICATIONS, LTD.
*World Leader In International Trade Publications,
Software & Online Education*
P.O. Box 337 • Allegan, MI 49010
Phone: 269-673-7242 • Fax: 269-673-5901 • email: inquiries@boskage.com
www.boskage.com • **888-880-4088**

EXPORT
COMPLIANCE
A Practical Guide To Licensing And Controls

INTRODUCTION

Have you ever wondered exactly how a country exerts its influence on another country? Through the use of U.S. export controls and embargos, countries like North Korea have felt the full force of U.S. dissatisfaction with their forms of leadership and nuclear proliferating activities. While this stance has received little response from these leaders, their populations remain economically and technologically malnourished. Many scholars of the Cold War cite U.S. and CoCom (Coordinating Committee for Multilateral Export Controls) denial of western technology to the former Soviet Union and its principal allies as contributing factors to the eventual demise of the Soviet Union. Today, export controls are used for a variety of purposes; namely, to protect U.S. economic vitality and national security. This is why you will find the products affected by U.S. export controls vary and the countries impacted by such controls to be ever-changing. There are stiff civil and criminal penalties for not adhering to these regulations. Whether you agree or disagree with the politics surrounding export controls, if you are involved in the business of exporting, it is mandatory you understand and implement required practices.

The purpose of this book is to give the beginning to intermediate U.S. export control practitioner the tools and resources to use and comply with the U.S. export controls with ease and care.

This book thoroughly discusses key regulations and addresses the export license application process step-by-step. Most individuals or corporations do not deal exclusively with one agency Department of State or Department of Commerce. This guide combines them both for the ease and complete comprehension of the reader. Figure A should give you a pretty good idea of the process we'll be taking you through as you read this book.

Upon completion of the book, the reader should know how to:

- Identify the type of product that requires a license,
- Select appropriate agencies in which to apply,
- Classify a product,
- Apply for a license,
- Find information in the ITAR/EAR faster,
- Recognize sanctions and embargoes and their impact on end-user screening, and
- Apply the information for instituting best practices for company compliance with U.S. export controls.

TABLE OF CONTENTS

APPENDIX

CHAPTER 1

COMMODITY JURISDICTION

Overview of U.S. Export Controls

Preceding the Export Control Act of 1949, controls on exports theoretically date back to the late 1700's. Congress in Philadelphia declared the importation of British goods to be illegal and later outlawed the export of goods to Great Britain. Since then, the United States has, for a variety of reasons, imposed export controls through legislation, such as the Embargo Act, the Trading with the Enemy Act, the Neutrality Act, and the Export Control Act. The effectiveness of these export regulations has been further improved by joining forces with other countries to further national security, nonproliferation and foreign policy interest - for example, the United States is currently a member of the Nuclear Suppliers Group, the Australia Group, the Missile Technology Control Regime, and the Wassenaar Arrangement. As a result, export control is a complex determining process, requiring the oversight of many different U.S. government agencies. As an exporter, it will be important for you to determine which government agency has jurisdiction over the products you export.

There are two major jurisdiction categories:

1. **The EAR**. As part of the U.S. Department of Commerce, the Bureau of Industry and Security controls the exports of both commercial and dual-use goods and services, as codified in the Export Administration Regulations (EAR), 15 CFR parts 730-774:

- **Commercial** goods and services.

- **Dual-use** goods and services.

2. **The ITAR.** Guided by the Arms Export Control Act, the Office of Defense Trade Controls (part of the U.S. Department of State) controls the exports of defense articles, services and technology within the United States Munitions List (USML) , as codified in the International Trade and Arms Regulations (ITAR, 22 CFR Parts 120-130).

When establishing the commodity jurisdiction of an article, this does not mean said product is subject to further control (such as a license). It simply establishes under which regulatory jurisdiction the article(s) and/or activities fall. The license determination process will be discussed in subsequent chapters. Commodity jurisdiction determination can be made two ways:

1. Self-determination, involving a thorough review of the product specifications and history and placing it under the appropriate government agency (or)

2. A request to the government for commodity jurisdiction determination.

The Export Control Act of 1949, which gave the U.S. Department of Commerce primary responsibility for administering and enforcing export controls on dual-use items, and, for the first time, defined three reasons for the imposition of these controls - national security, foreign policy, and short supply.

EAR Commodity Jurisdiction

The EAR defines **exports** as "…actual shipment or transmission of items subject to the EAR out of the United States, or release of technology or software subject to the EAR to a foreign national in the United States…" (EAR 734.2(b))

The EAR applies to:

- U.S. origin commercial items including hardware, software and technology.
- Dual-use items with commercial and military application.
- Reexported EAR goods from one foreign country to another foreign country.
- Release of technology or software that is subject to the EAR, to a foreign national.
- Certain activities of a U.S. person related to proliferation of nuclear devices, chemicals, biological weapons, missiles and technology.
- U.S. or foreign person prohibited by an order under the EAR and technical assistance to a foreign person with respect to U.S. encryption commodities and software.
- Certain commodities produced by any plant located outside of the U.S. that is a direct product of the use of U.S. origin, technology or software. It also includes export of certain foreign made items produced from U.S. origin technology.

It is important to know if a product is of U.S. origin when making a jurisdiction decision. Obviously, a product not of U.S. origin does not need an export control under the EAR. Origin can be easily determined in most cases, especially when the product in question is made in the United States exclusively from U.S. components. The EAR defines U.S. origin in section 734.3 as:

- Products manufactured in the U.S.
- U.S. origin parts, components, materials or other commodities even if integrated abroad into foreign made products are U.S. origin.
- U.S. origin software commingled with foreign software.
- U.S. origin technology commingled with foreign technology.
- Articles that have entered the U.S. and then have been exported from the U.S., including articles within a Foreign Trade Zone as well as those moving in transit through the U.S. from one foreign country to another.

However, sometimes it is less obvious whether or not a product is of U.S. origin. If U.S. parts or components are exported and then incorporated into a final product outside of the U.S., the reexport may still be subject to the EAR. To determine if a product for reexport is subject to U.S. licensing requirements, one must determine if the U.S. content is below a certain level known as *de minimis*. Depending on the percentage value of U.S. content versus foreign content, a license for reexport may or may not be required. Examples include:

- Reexported products containing over 10% "controlled" U.S. origin and going to a terrorist-supporting country such as North Korea, Cuba, Iran, Sudan, or Syria will require a license.
- The product does not meet the *de minimis* U.S. value content of below 10% , or

- Reexported products with over 25% "controlled" U.S. origin will require an export license when shipped to most countries.

In calculating *de minimis* U.S. content, only calculate the value, parts, components, or materials that are subject to a license i.e. "controlled". It is not always necessary to calculate *de minimis* requirements if the U.S. components does not require a license. For further details on calculating values according to *de minimis* rules, please refer to Supplement no. 2 of part 734 of EAR.

EXAMPLE: *DE MINIMIS* CALCULATION

All the components for Product A cost $50. The cost of the U.S. controlled components is $15. The sales price for the Product A is $100.   The percentage value of the U.S. origin "controlled" material is 15% (15 divided by 100). This means the product is exempt from license requirements for most countries because it is below the 25% requirement. However, the same product requires a license if it is to be reexported to a terrorist-supporting country, because its value content is above the 10% requirement.

Some articles have no *de minimis* requirements. (This is explained in more detail in the EAR section 734.4.) However, the exporter may need to anticipate complications rising from situations in which the article will be reexported from another country with embargo restrictions not corresponding with the U.S. embargo restrictions, or where *de minimis* requirements apply.

EXAMPLE: NO *DE MINIMIS* CALCULATION

A product is exported from the U.S. without the need for a license to France. The same product is reexported from France to a Country C. Country C does not have any trade restrictions with France; however, there are trade restrictions between Country

C and the U.S. It is important that the U.S. shipper know the *de minimis* level of the product. In this instance, if the level of the U.S.-controlled content is above the *de minimis* the reexport to country C is a violation of the EAR.

The EAR does **not** cover some of the goods regulated by the following agencies. Commodities under the jurisdiction of other agencies such as:

- *Department of State*: Licenses defense services and defense munitions articles, which are covered in the ITAR.

- *Department of the Treasury, Office of Foreign Assets Control (OFAC):* administers and enforces economic and trade sanctions against target foreign countries.

- *Nuclear Regulatory Commission, Office of International Programs*: Licenses nuclear material and equipment.

- *Department of Energy, Office of Arms Controls and Non-Proliferation, Export Control Division*: Licenses nuclear technology and technical data for nuclear power and special nuclear materials.

- *Department of Energy: Office of Fuel Programs*: Licenses natural gas and electric power.

- *Patent and Trademark Office*: Licensing and Review: Oversees patent filing data sent abroad.

- *Drug Enforcement Administration*: Oversees export of controlled substances.

- *Food and Drug Administration*: Regulates medical devices and drugs.

Nor does the EAR control these specific goods:

- Prerecorded phonograph reproducing printed books, pamphlets and miscellaneous publications including newspapers, periodicals, books etc.

- Information that is accessible to the public in the form of technology, software, books, periodicals, open patent applications available at the patent office, open conference meetings, seminars and trade shows.

- Fundamental research, basic and applied research in science and engineering that is ordinarily published and known amongst the scientific community.

- Educational information, if released in catalog courses and teaching laboratories of academic institutions.

ITAR Commodity Jurisdiction

ITAR is primarily governed by the Arms Export Control Act, 22 U.S.C. 2778 and Executive Order 11958, as amended. The Arms Export Control Act (AECA) gives the President authority to control the export of defense articles and service while the Executive Order 11958 gives the Secretary of State power. The statutes of the AECA can be found in the United States Code, Title 22-Foreign Relations and Chapter 39– Arms Export Control. ITAR executes the terms of the AECA and Executive Order that controls exports of *defense articles, technical data* and *defense services*.

The term *defense article* refers to any item that is specifically designed, developed, configured, adapted or modified for a military application. This definition can assist with discerning between "dual use" military/civil stipulations of the EAR and the military application stipulations of the ITAR. The ITAR definition focuses on the original intent of the article. Therefore, knowing the history of the product is important when determining jurisdiction. There are two questions to consider.

1. Was the article originally designed, developed, configured, for a military purpose? If the answer is "yes", the jurisdiction, depending on other facts, may fall under the Department of State.

2. Was the article later modified for military/defense specifications? If yes, it may also fall under the Department of State.

> *T*IP! It is worth adding the intended use of the article after it has been exported while applying for a license can not be a factor when determining jurisdiction or when classifying a product. Example: If you ship a missile for the purpose of decorative display in someone's living room, it would still fall under the Department of State even though it is not being used for military purposes.

Technical data is defined as information that is required for the design, development, production, manufacture, assembly, operation, repair, testing, maintenance or modification of a defense article. Information can be in the physical form of items like blueprints, drawings or instructions.

A *defense service* is the furnishing of assistance to a foreign person, whether in U.S. or abroad, with the design, development, manufacture, engineering, production, assembly, testing, repair, maintenance, modification of U.S. defense articles. The transmission of technical data can be accomplished by phone, email, training, conference or correspondence to a foreign national. This type of activity is still regulated by the Department of State (ITAR).

These activities and regulations will be further discussed in subsequent chapters.

If commodity jurisdiction still cannot be determined independently, a written request to the Directorate of Defense Trade Controls (DDTC) in Washington, DC can be sent with supporting documentation that addresses the following:

- Product details/description.
- History/origin of your commodity that addresses what the item was originally designed for and if it was modified later for military/civil use. Also, indicate whether the article was funded by a U.S. government agency at any time.
- Current use, with supporting documentation of commercial or military sales data.
- Special characteristics such as performance specifications.

Note: A response to a commodity jurisdiction request can take approximately 65 days. Please see Fig. 1 on the next page for a Commodity Jurisdiction Question Chart. If you answer "yes" to one or more questions in the same column, your article most likely falls under that jurisdiction.

Penalties

Penalties for non-compliance with U.S. export controls include:

VIOLATIONS UNDER EAR JURISDICTION

- Individual criminal penalties for willful violations of up to $250,000, or imprisonment for up to ten years, or both, for each violation.

DEPARTMENT OF COMMERCE (EAR)	DEPARTMENT OF STATE (ITAR)
• Has the product been used commercially?	• Has the product been used commercially?
• Does it have commercial specifications?	• Does the performance equivalence of your product meet military standards or applications?
• Can the article be used for commercial and military applications, although NOT originally intended for military applications or for weapons, military related use or design?	• Was the article originally designed for military applications and intended for military purposes?
• Is the article a commercial product not regulated by another governmental agency?	• Is the technical data military in scope and not publicly available or widely known?
• Does it have predominant civil applications?	• Was product development or modification funded by a government agency?

Fig. 1

- Individual criminal penalties for knowing violations of up to the greater of $50,000, or five times the value of the exports or imprisonment for up to five years, or both, for each violation.

- Corporate criminal penalties for willful violations of up to the greater of $1,000,000 or five times the value of the exports for each violation.

- Corporate criminal penalties for knowing violations of up to the greater of $50,000 or five times the value of the exports for each violation.

- Administrative penalties for each violation, including denial of export privileges.

VIOLATIONS UNDER ITAR JURISDICTION

- Administrative debarment from participating in the export of defense articles

- Civil penalties not to exceed $500,000 for each violation involving controls imposed on the export of defense articles and defense services.

- Criminal penalties not to exceed $1,000,000 for each violation, imprisonment not more than 10 years, or both for transactions with countries supporting acts of international terrorism under Sec. 2780.

In the unfortunate event that an export violation occurs prior to the applicable governmental agency discovery, agencies such as the BIS and DDTC recommend submitting a written voluntary disclosure to the BIS or DDTC immediately after the violation is discovered.

The written notification for an ITAR voluntary disclosure should include:

- Detailed description of the violation.

- Circumstances surrounding the violation.

- All individuals and addresses of person(s) suspected of being involved in the violation.

- Product description and USML category number.

- Contact person of the individual making prior disclosure.

- Mitigating circumstances such as whether violation was accidental.

- Any supporting documentation.

- Certification that all information is true and correct.

For specifics of voluntary disclosure notification, read 127.12 (c) (2) of ITAR. If the initial notification does not contain all of the required information listed above within 60 calendar days, the voluntary disclosure will be disqualified.

The decision to submit a voluntary disclosure should not be taken lightly. Ideally, legal counsel should be consulted. A voluntary disclosure does not preclude a company or individual from penalties, although in many instances the penalty may be reduced.

REFERENCES AND RESOURCES

International Traffic and Arms Regulations (22 CFR)

Export Administration Regulations (15 CFR)

The Arms Export Control Act (Chapter 39)

Directorate of Defense Trade Controls (http://www.pmddtc. state.gov/)

Bureau of Industry and Security (www.bis.doc.gov)

CHAPTER 2

CLASSIFICATION OF MERCHANDISE

Now that we have established jurisdiction of the articles, it is time to determine if a license is required. Figuring out whether the article requires an export license should be broken down systematically, otherwise one can easily get lost in the many parts of the EAR or ITAR. Let's review what worked for many of us in school, i.e., using catchy sentences to remember information for a test or quiz. Let's use the first word of a sentence to remember the **EAR** export license identification process.

Can't Give Culprits Capabilities to be Lunatics

These letters each stand for a step in the export license identification process:

1. Classify
2. General Prohibitions
3. Commerce Control
4. Country Chart
5. License Exceptions

It is in the above order that this book directs the reader to approach the license determination process under the EAR. Subsequent sections will cover each step in turn, but in this chapter, we'll deal with Step 1: Classification.

EAR Commodity Classification Process

The importance of classifying the article correctly cannot be stressed enough. Classifying the article means determining the correct Export Control Classification Number (ECCN). The ECCN indicates what controls are placed on a certain article, and if those controls require a license prior to shipment. If the ECCN is wrong, the individual or corporation is still liable for the domino effect of the consequences that may occur due to incorrect classifications. If the article is something the applicant does not produce, requesting the ECCN from the manufacturer is highly recommended. In the event the manufacturer does not know or have the ECCN, obtain as much information on the product as possible from engineers, chemists, or others in order to self-classify. For technical articles, the classifier should work together with engineers or other individuals who are familiar with the technical specifications of the article If all else fails, another option is to submit a formal classification request to the BIS. Instructions for that process will be covered in a separate section.

> *T*IP! *If you are a distributor or otherwise not the manufacturer when requesting the ECCN, get it in writing with signature.* **See Vendor Product Export Control Questionnaire template (Appendix N)**. *Feel free to tailor the questions to the applicable industry.*

The ECCN is five-character alphanumeric code. The example below will be used frequently as we discuss the classification process.

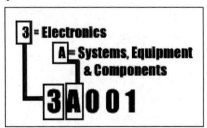

FIG. 2 Source: BIS website

EXAMPLE:

The applicant is a manufacturer of gas turbine engines for civilian airplanes. The engine propulsion settings are consistent for use in civil aircraft. The engine does not contain parts that can be used for military or nuclear purposes.

STEP 1

Determine the ECCN by utilizing the Commerce Control List (CCL). Essentially, the CCL is a list of goods controlled by the EAR. The list of controlled goods is identified by a five-character alphanumeric classification – this alphanumeric **is** the ECCN. The CCL can be found in **Supplement 1 to Part 774** of the EAR. The CCL contains the following 10 categories:

0	Nuclear Materials, Facilities, and Equipment (and Miscellaneous Items)
1	Materials, Chemicals, Microorganism and Toxins
2	Materials Processing
3	Electronics
4	Computers
5	Telecommunications and Information Security
6	Lasers and Sensors
7	Navigation and Avionics
8	Marine
9	**Propulsion Systems, Space Vehicles and Related Equipment (Aerospace and Propulsion)**

Fig. 3

In our example using the gas turbine engine, "9" will be the first number of the ECCN.

9 _ _ _ _

STEP 2

Referring to EAR Part 738 (b), you must select the product group the article falls under. This time the equivalents are alphabetical. The groups are as follows:

A	**Systems, Equipment and Components**
B	Test, Inspection and Production Equipment
C	Material
D	Software
E	Technology

Fig. 4

Continuing with the example of the gas turbine engine, **"A"** is correct, because it is identified with systems, equipment or components. Thus far, the ECCN for turbine gas engine is **9A**. We're almost there. If you still experience difficulty, look in the **Alphabetical Index of the Commerce Control List** for a quick hint. For example, let's pretend the article is "bacteria". Luckily, "bacteria" is found on page 4 of the Index with a suggested ECCN of 1C354.a. (As a disclaimer, this index is not a panacea. It does not contain every product nor should you assume the classification it gives is instantly applicable to the article. However, it can be utilized as a starting point, followed by thoroughly reading through the categories of the product.)

Our classification so far is:

9A _ _ _

STEP 3

With the first two characters identified as "9A", go to the Commerce Control List **Part 774 Supplement 1**. This is where knowledge of the product becomes important, because now you must read the various options within this section and pick the classification that best fits the product. In our example, there are many choices in the 9A section, where you will read choices such as space launch vehicles (9A004) and sound rockets (9A104); however, these options definitely don't fit our product. The correct answer for our product is:

9A991 "Aircraft", i.e., and gas turbine engines not controlled by 9A001 or 9A101 and parts and components, i.e.

Now let's see why this is our classification. What do the last three digits mean?

9 – Category

A – Product Group

9 – Reason for Control

9 – Relates to Reasons for Control

1 – Used for Numerical Ordering only

While it is not necessary to know what the coding means for the last three characters in order to classify, it provides helpful context; therefore, the purpose for the last three characters is discussed below. (738 EAR).

The third character indicates reasons for control (see Fig. 5 on the next page):

0	National Security Reasons
1	Missile Technology
2	Nuclear Nonproliferation
3	Chemical & Biological Weapons
4-8	Currently not used
9	Anti-terrorism, Crime Control, Regional Stability, Short Supply, UN Sanctions etc.

Fig. 5

The fourth character indicates whether a product is controlled due to (1) multilateral or (2) unilateral controls. Unilateral controls are imposed only by the U.S. government, while multilateral controls are agreed upon controls imposed by countries that are members of a particular organization or control regime. An example of a unilateral control is U.S. embargo against Cuba. A multilateral control example is the Nuclear Supplier Group, with a membership of 40 countries dedicated to ceasing the proliferation of nuclear weapons.

Using the example 9A991, the "9" in the third slot indicates controlbased on concerns over Anti-Terrorism, Crime Control, Regional Stability, Short Supply, UN Sanctions. The "9" in the fourth slot explains the reason for this control is unilateral. The last digit is simply the sequential numbering of the ECCN within its category.

STEP 4

If the article doesn't fit any of the categories, yet is subject to the EAR, there is a good possibility it falls under the classification of EAR99. In fact, many commercial items are classified under this heading. EAR99 is commonly referred to as the "catch-all basket" because if the commodity or technology does not fall under any other agency or jurisdiction, then it belongs under the EAR.

However, if there is no specified ECCN for the article in the CCL, the default classification is EAR99.

If the ECCN still cannot be found, or if you are unsure of the classification, let the BIS do the hard work for you by submitting a request for ECCN classification. A commodity classification request can be submitted through the BIS's automated interface, the Simplified Network Application Process Redesign (SNAP-R). Remember, a response may take as long as 2-3 months; however, this could be the safest and most compliant approach. Go to the BIS website at http:///www.bis.doc.gov/licensing/cclrequest guidance.html to find guidelines for requesting a commodity classification.

ITAR Commodity Classification Process

If your items are on the USML list, determining whether or not those items require a license is fairly easy, considering that approximately 95% of the items on the USML require a license.

In almost all cases, items on the USML will need an export license. Go to 22 CFR 121.1 of the ITAR for a detailed list of the USML provisions. Remember, a USML article is article or service specifically designed, developed, configured, adapted or modified for a military application. A chart containing the categories of the USML is provided in Fig. 6 (see next page).

In classifying a USML product, let's use the example of a gas turbine engine that is designed specifically for a gas turbine on a *military* helicopter frame. This article would fall under Category VIII section category (j). Below is an excerpt from that portion of the USML.

(j) Components, parts, accessories, attachments, and associated equipment (including ground support equipment) specifically designed or modified for the articles in paragraphs (a) through (i) of this category, excluding aircraft tires and propellers used with reciprocating engines.

I	Firearms, Close Assault Weapons and Combat Shotguns	V	Explosives and Energetic Materials, Propellants, Incendiary Agents and their constituents.
II	Guns and Armament	VI	Vessels of War and Special Naval Equipment
III	Ammunition/Ordinance	VIII	Aircraft and Associated Equipment
IV	Launch Vehicles, Guided Missiles, Ballistic Missiles, rockets Torpedoes, Bombs and Mines	IX	Military Training Personnel Equipment
XVI	Nuclear Weapons, Design and Testing Related Items	XIX	(Reserved)
XVII	Classified Articles, Technical Data, and Defense Services not otherwise enumerated	XX	Submersible Vessels, Oceanographic and Associated Equipment
XVIII	Directed Energy Weapons	XXI	Miscellaneous Articles
XIX	Directed Energy Weapons		

Fig. 6

The USML is not confined only to defense articles (which many may interpret as tangible products, hardware or articles), but also includes technical data and services. Technical data includes any information that assists in the design, development, production, manufacture assembly operation, repair, testing, maintenance, or modification of articles controlled in the USML. Therefore, when technical data is exported outside of the U.S., whether physically or within the U.S. via a foreign national, it is considered a permanent export, requiring an export license applied through a DSP-5 and a Technical Assistance Agreement (TAA). These requirements will be discussed in further detail in Chapter 6.

The restrictions on sharing controlled technical data also apply to defense services. A defense service is defined as giving assistance, training or technical information to foreign persons whether it is done in the U.S. or abroad. This pertains to the service, maintenance, design development production, testing or modification, and/or assembly of a U.S. controlled item. An export can occur on U.S. soil in various ways. The most common methods include:

- Verbal - from a U.S. citizen to a foreign national.
- Written- email or reading of technical documents.
- Visual- site visits.

This topic will be covered in more detail in Chapter 7.

This concludes our chapter on classification of merchandise for export. Please note, you can also look at Appendix A for a flowchart of the license process.

EXERCISE

You have two orders for customers in Denmark and Hong Kong who would like to purchase electronic computer components. These components will only be used for civil-end use purposes and will not be diverted to another country contrary to the Export Administration Regulations.

What is the classification of this product?

What are the reasons for control?

ANSWER:

1. 4A001

2. National Security Column 2, Missile Technology
Column 1

REFERENCES

International Traffic and Arms Regulations (22 CFR)

Export Administration Regulations (15 CFR)

CHAPTER 3

DO I NEED AN EXPORT LICENSE?

In Chapter 2, we learned how to classify. In this chapter, we will learn how to determine if an export license is required.

On the subject of export licenses, the difference between EAR vs. ITAR jusidiction is dramatic. If your commodity falls under ECCN (EAR) jurisdiction, the chances that you may need to apply for a license are far less than if your commodity falls under the jurisdiction of the USML (ITAR). BIS estimates that only 3.6% of U.S trade was potentially impacted upon by the EAR. A large volume of these licenses are for controlled items for end-use in China. In contrast, while the exact number is not known, items controlled under ITAR will require a license in most instances.

In the last chapter, we covered the first of these steps. In this chapter, we'll cover the other four. Let's start with Step 2, General Prohibitions. Once again, let's use the first letter of each word of a sentence to remember the EAR export license identification process.

Can't Give Culprits Capabilities to be Lunatics

1. **C**lassify
2. **G**eneral Prohibitions
3. **C**ommerce Control
4. **C**ountry Chart
5. **L**icense Exceptions

Review General Prohibitions

Now it's time to review the general prohibitions to determine exporter's responsibilities when exporting or reexporting under the EAR. Before you go through the General Prohibitions to figure out which prohibition applies to their article and ensure they are in compliance with the provision, asking the following questions will help determine which prohibitions may apply to the article.

1. What is the item?

2. Where is it going?

3. Who is involved?

4. What will the product be used for?

In brief, General Prohibitions 1-3 describe an exporter's obligations under the **EAR**.

- **General Prohibition 1-** Prohibits export or reexport of a U.S. controlled item under the EAR to another country without a license or license exception.

- **General Prohibition 2-** Prohibits the reexport and/or export of articles that have more than the *de minimis* amount of controlled U.S. content.

- **General Prohibition 3-** A license is required for exports or reexports to Cuba or countries in the Country Group D:1 chart.

General Prohibitions 4-10 describe certain activities that are not allowed without **BIS** authorization.

- **General Prohibition 4-** Prohibits actions ruled out by a denial order.

- **General Prohibition 5-** Prohibits exports or reexport to prohibited end-uses or end-users.

- **General Prohibition 6-** Prohibits exports or reexports to embargoed destinations.

- **General Prohibition 7-** Prohibits support of proliferation activities by U.S. persons.

- **General Prohibition 8-** Prohibits an in transit shipment to countries specified in paragraph (b) (8) (ii) 736 of EAR.

- **General Prohibition 9-** License or license exception cannot be violated.

- **General Prohibition 10-** Prohibits transactions if an individual/corporation has knowledge that a violation.

Review Commerce Control List (CCL)

The information we gain from next two steps will determine if the article is controlled or not. If controlled, the article will require a license or a license exemption in order to be exported. **The first of the two steps is to establish the reason for control.** This can be done by going to the section of the Commerce Control List that applies to the product or technology. Using the example of Fig. 7 on the following page, showing the CCL listing for the classification of 9A991, go to category 9 of Part 774 of the EAR.

9A991 "Aircraft", n.e.s., and gas turbine engines not controlled by 9A001 or 9A101 and parts and components, n.e.s.

License Requirements

Reason for Control: AT, UN

Control(s)   Country Chart

AT applies to entire entry   AT Column 1

UN applies to 9A991.a   Iraq, North Korea, and Rwanda

License Requirement Notes: There is no de minimis level for foreign-made aircraft described by this entry that incorporate commercial primary or standby instrument systems that integrate QRS11-00100-100/101 or commercial automatic flight control systems that integrate QRS11-00050-443/569 Micromachined Angular Rate Sensors (see §734.4(a) of the EAR).

License Exceptions

    LVS: N/A
    GBS: N/A
    CIV: N/A

List of Items Controlled

Unit: Number
Related Controls: QRS11 Micromachined Angular Rate Sensors are subject to the export licensing jurisdiction of the U.S. Department of State, Directorate of Defense Trade Controls, unless the QRS11-00100-100/101 is integrated into and included as an integral part of a commercial primary or standby instrument system of the type described in ECCN 7A994, or aircraft of the type described in ECCN that incorporates such a system, or is exported solely for integration into such a system; or the QRS11-00050-443/569 is integrated into an automatic flight control system of the type described in ECCN 7A994, or aircraft of the type described in ECCN that incorporates such a system, or are exported solely for integration into such a system. (See Commodity Jurisdiction requirements in 22 CFR Part 121; Category VIII(e), Note(1)) In the latter case, such items are subject to the licensing jurisdiction of the Department of Commerce. Technology specific to the development and production of QRS11 sensors remains subject to the licensing jurisdiction of the Department of State.
    Related Definitions: N/A
    Items:

Fig. 7

These sections must be read carefully and thoroughly. A dedicated reading of this chapter will inform you that there are no license exceptions, as indicated by the "N/A" indication next to the listed exception categories. Further reading indicates that even if the article is a commercial or civil aircraft, if it contains a QRS11 micro machine angular rate sensor, the article falls under the jurisdiction of the

Department of State. The QRS11 reference was added after the lengthy debate between an aerospace corporation and Department of State. The aerospace company agreed to pay approximately $15 million to settle charges that it illegally exported a commercial aircraft that contained QRS-11 gyro chip to China and State agreed to add this disclaimer to the regulations for clarification purposes. It was essentially a jurisdiction battle with the aerospace company, which argued that it was under the jurisdiction of EAR and the State asserting it was under their jurisdiction. Eventually the company paid the fines and worked out the arrangement that the QRS-11 chip would be specifically mentioned on the US Munitions List. Other large exporters also suffered the same headache over the QRS-11 issue and paid sizeable penalties. You can benefit from the lessons learned by these companies who paid the price for failing to comply with the conditions of the CCL. The bottom line? **Read the CCL notations carefully.**

Let's return to our example using the ECCN classification "9A991". In the License Requirements section of classification 9A991, it states the reason for control is for AT (Anti-Terrorism). UN (United Nations) is a reason given for control if the ECCN is 9A991.a, but since our classification is only 9A991 and not 9A991.a, only the AT column 1 applies to our article. Other abbreviations for reasons for control are as follows:

CB: Chemical & Biological Weapons

CC: Crime Control

CW: Chemical Weapons Convention

EI: Encryption Items

FC: Firearms Convention

MT: Missile TechnologNS: National Security

NP: Nuclear Nonproliferation

RS: Regional Stability

SS: Short Supply

SI: Significant Items

SL: Surreptitious Listening

Review Country Commerce Chart:

Supplement No. 1 Part 738, shown on Fig. 8 on the following page, is the Commerce Country Chart. This chart breaks down countries and provides the reason for controls in each column. If controlled, the reason will be indicated with an "X" in the row for the applicable country and in the column representing the abbreviated control. Review the sample on the next page from the EAR.

EXAMPLE:

Let's suppose that we are exporting our product with an ECCN of 9A991 to India. The reason for control is AT Column 1. There is no X in the cell in the India row. Therefore, no license is required to ship this article to India. If no license is required, you could proceed to ship it under NLR, i.e., No License Required. If there was an "X" in the column on the row for India, however, a license would be required. Even if that were the case, though, we still wouldn't be done. We'd want to make sure that we checked our product for license exemptions.

Check For License Exceptions

From the Commerce Control List and Country Chart, you have discovered whether the product requires a license. Before going through the arduous process of applying for an export license, however, go to Part 740 of EAR, and see if the article qualifies for one of the license exceptions found there.

The summary that follows is a brief overview of the various license exceptions available under the EAR. As with most regulations, there are conditions, conditions and more conditions to be met. So before declaring, "I have license exceptions!", read all the conditions found in 740.2 to ensure you are in full compliance with the regulations.

Commerce Country Chart

Countries	Chemical & Biological Weapons			Nuclear Nonproliferation		National Security		Missile Tech	Regional Stability		Firearms Convention	Crime Control			Anti-Terrorism	
	CB 1	CB 2	CB 3	NP 1	NP 2	NS 1	NS 2	MT 1	RS 1	RS 2	FC 1	CC 1	CC 2	CC 3	AT 1	AT 2
Grenada	X	X		X		X	X	X	X	X	X	X		X		
Guatemala	X	X		X		X	X	X	X	X	X	X		X		
Guinea	X	X		X		X	X	X	X	X		X		X		
Guinea-Bissau	X	X		X		X	X	X	X	X		X		X		
Guyana	X	X		X		X	X	X	X	X	X	X		X		
Haiti	X	X		X		X	X	X	X	X	X	X		X		
Honduras	X	X		X		X	X	X	X	X	X	X		X		
Hong Kong	X	X		X		X		X	X	X		X		X		
Hungary	X					X		X	X							
Iceland	X			X		X		X	X							
India	X	X	X	X		X	X	X	X	X		X		X		
Indonesia	X	X		X		X	X	X	X	X		X		X		
Iran	See part 746 of the EAR to determine whether a license is required in order to export or reexport to this destination.															
Iraq[1]	X	X	X	X	X	X	X	X	X	X		X	X	X		

FIG. 8

If one of the codes shown below is listed in the exception area of your product's CCL entry, a license exception may apply for your product, which will mean that you do not need to apply for an export license. Here are the license exceptions with a brief explanation of their meanings, along with. the qualifications that your export must also meet if your CCL entry has the corresponding exception code.

Limited Value Shipments (LVS): This exception authorizes export or reexport of a single shipment of certain commodities if the selling price value does not exceed a certain limit. For example, within ECCN 9A002 (see Fig. 9) is the License exception LVS: $5,000. This allows the shipment of this article without applying for license, if the value of the single shipment is under $5,000, and it is going to a country in the Group B category. (Group B countries can be found in Supplement 1 to part 740.)

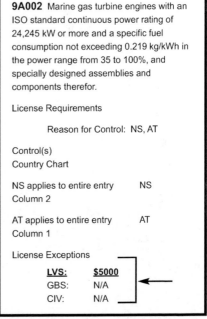

9A002 Marine gas turbine engines with an ISO standard continuous power rating of 24,245 kW or more and a specific fuel consumption not exceeding 0.219 kg/kWh in the power range from 35 to 100%, and specially designed assemblies and components therefor.

License Requirements

Reason for Control: NS, AT

Control(s)
Country Chart

NS applies to entire entry   NS
Column 2

AT applies to entire entry   AT
Column 1

License Exceptions
 LVS: **$5000**
 GBS: N/A
 CIV: N/A

Fig. 9

Group B Countries (GBS): In order to qualify for a GBS exemption, your product must be (1) going to a country found in the Group B Country List (Part 740 EAR), (2) have licensing reason code NS (National Security), and (3) be classified under an ECCN that shows "GBS: YES" in the CCL exemption listing.

Civil End-Users (CIV): In order to qualify for a CIV exemption, your product must (1) be destined for civil end-use, (2) be going to a country fond on Country List Group D, (3) have licensing reason code NS, (4) under no circumstances be going to North Korea and (5) be classified under an ECCN that shows "CIV: YES" in the CCL exemption listing.

Technology and Software Under Restriction (TSR): In order to qualify for a TSR exemption, your product must (1) be an export or reexport of technology and software (2) be restricted for NS reasons, and (3) be classified under an ECCN that shows "TSR: YES" in the CCL exemption listing, provided that a written assurance from the importer is required, testifying the technology or software will not go to countries in Group D:1 or E:2 as well as other assurances.

Adjusted Peak Performance - Computers (APP): In order to qualify for an APP exemption, your product must (1) be either a computer or assembly under ECCN 4A003, or else technology or software under 4D001 or 4E001, (2) be going to a computer tier country stipulated in 740.7 (c) of EAR, and (3) be classified under an ECCN that shows "APP: YES" in the CCL exemption listing.

Key Management Infrastructure (KMI): In order to qualify for a KMI exemption, your product must (1) be encryption software and equipment, (2) not be from any countries in Group E:1, and (3) be classified under an ECCN that shows "KMI: YES" in the CCL exemption listing.

Temporary Imports, Exports, and Reexports (TMP): In order to qualify for a TMP exemption, your product must (1) be a commodity or software for certain temporary situations (for example, "tools of trade" for temporary use abroad by U.S. persons or employees assigned abroad, exhibition and demonstration articles), or (2) be a temporary export to a U.S. subsidiary, affiliate or facility in Country Group B, and (3) be classified under an ECCN that shows "TMP: YES" in the CCL exemption listing.

Servicing and Replacement of Parts and Equipment (RPL): A license exception applies if your product (1) is a "one-for-one" replacement of parts or equipment, and (2) is classified under an ECCN that shows "RPL: YES" in the CCL exemption listing..

Governments, International Organizations, and International Inspections Under The Chemical Weapons Convention (GOV): This provision allows exports and reexports of international nuclear safeguards to the above organizations if the export in question is classified under an ECCN that shows "GOV: YES" in the CCL exemption listing.

Gift Parcels and Humanitarian Donations (GFT): In order to qualify for a GFT exemption, your product must be (1) a gift parcel by an individual, religious, charitable or educational organization, (2) not for the purpose of sale, and (3) classified under an ECCN that shows "GFT: YES" in the CCL exemption listing.

Technology and Software Unrestricted (TSU): No license is required for exports and reexports of operation technology and software that would be considered publicly available.

Baggage (BAG): No license is required for eligible software, technology, commodity or personal baggage for U.S. persons temporarily traveling aboard or for a long-term move abroad.

Aircraft and Vessels (AVS): Foreign registered civil aircraft on a temporary sojourn in the U.S. and U.S civil aircraft for temporary sojourn abroad do not require export licenses.

Additional Permissive Reexports (APR): In order to qualify for an APR exemption, your product must be (1) from Country Group A:1 or from cooperating countries that is not controlled for NP, CB, MT, SI or CC reasons, or (2) from Country Group A:1. and being reexported to a country in Group B that is not also included in Country Group D:2, D:3 or D:4; Cambodia or Laos, and (3) classified under an ECCN that shows "GFT: YES" in the CCL exemption listing.

Encryption Commodities and Software (ENC): A license exception is available for ECCN 5A002.a.1. .a.2, etc provided they do not meet mass-market criteria of the Cryptography Note.

Agricultural Commodities (AGR): This provision allows the export and reexport of agricultural commodities to Cuba.

ITAR License Identification

Most items that fall under the USML require a license; therefore, it usually takes an exemption for a license not to be required. Like the EAR, ITAR also contains many exemptions found throughout its text available to the exporter. A brief summary of some of the most commonly used exemptions includes:

123.4	Temporary Import license exemptions
123.4(a)(1)	Temporary imports of classified U.S. goods for purposes of pair, warrant service or one for one placement

123.4 (a)(3)   Imported for purposes of exhibition, demonstration or marketing in the U.S. and subsequently returned

125.5   Exemption for plant visits

126.5   Permits the export or temporary import of unclassified articles or tech data to Canada for end use in Canada by Canadian citizens, or for return to the U.S without the need for a license. The exemption has various requirements and exemptions, found in ITAR 126.4 (a), 126.5 (b) and 126.5 (c). If one of these exemptions does apply, please be sure to identify the exemption you are claiming prior to time of export, using the Automated Export System (AES). The abbreviation for Canadian exemption is "CA", and the applicable exemption reference i.e. "22 CFR 126.5.(a)". Pay close attention to the limitations of this exemption for defense articles and related technical data and defense services. There is a list of approximately 21 items that do not apply in section 126.5(b)(1) to (21), so prior to using this exemption, it is highly suggested you read the exceptions.

EXERCISE:

You have two orders for customers in Denmark and Hong Kong who would like to purchase electronic computer components ECCN 4A001 controlled for National Security Column 2, Missile Technology Column 1. These components will only be used for civil end use purposes and will not be diverted to another country contrary to the Export Administration Regulations.

1. Utilizing the Commerce Control List and Country Chart, determine if a license is required for this product.

    Denmark

    Hong Kong

2. Are there any License exceptions for this product?

ANSWERS:

1. Denmark: Yes license required

   Hong Kong: Yes, license required

2. Yes, LVS if the classification is 4A001.a and the commodity value is under $5,000

We've now covered the process by which you make a distinction of jurisdiction between EAR and ITAR, classification of merchandise, and determination of required export licensing. Now, let's look at the process you need to go through in order to apply for export licenses when they are needed.

CHAPTER 4

GETTING STARTED: LICENSE REGISTRATION

Getting Started With BIS/EAR

SNAP-R is the system for submitting and tracking Export License Applications. It is available at no cost to the exporting community. With SNAP-R, you can:

- Submit export and reexport applications faster, as well as commodity classification requests via the Internet.

- Attach supporting documentation.

- Check status of an application.

To receive SNAP-R access, submit a letter containing company's name, address, telephone number and contact person/details.

BIS will send you a form, known as a "certification," which you'll need to fill out. After sending the completed certification back, you may be approved by BIS to submit applications electronically.

Upon approval, you will obtain a company identification number and PIN number that should be kept confidential and used to apply for licenses.

Getting Started With DDTC/ITAR

While getting started with BIS is free, getting started with the DDTC is a bit more involved and (as we'll see) requires payment of a fee. Before application for license can take place, the company (in other words., the manufacturer, exporter or broker of any defense articles, services or related technology) must be registered with the DDTC, even if that company does not export. When explaining the registration process, the government informs the registrant that registration does not give them the right to export but merely the right to request approval to export.

The first step toward registration with DDTC is to download Form DS-2032, Registration as Exporter, Manufacturer, or Broker, at the Department of State website. With your completed form, include the transmittal letter **(see Appendix L)**, as well as any supporting documentation such as:

- State Incorporation Certificate.
- State Certificate of Good Standing.
- State, County or City Business License.
- State Articles of Incorporation, sole proprietorship, partnerships, limited liability partnership/company, and corporations.

This is also a good time to select an "empowered official" for the company. Do so with care. The empowered official selected should understand ITAR provisions. As empowered official, he or she is now authorized to sign and process license applications on behalf of the company. It is recommended the empowered official be a senior official within the company with the authority to inquire into aspects of any export transaction and refuse to sign a license application, when necessary.

Note: the empowered official can be held liable for ITAR violations. This is another difference between the BIS process and that of the DDTC. It is not necessary to appoint an empowered official or designated signature to license application when applying through SNAP-R.

DDTC Registration Fees

A fee must be submitted to DDTC as part of the registration package. The registration fee was increased in 2008 and is currently based on a three-tier registration schedule (See Fig. 10).

- The first tier is a set fee of $2,250 per year for registrants who are renewing a registration, as well as those registering with the Department for the first time.

- The second tier is set at $2,750 per year, to be paid by those registrants for whom DDTC has reviewed, adjudicated or issued a response to between one and ten applications during the twelve-month period ending 90 days prior to the expiration of their current registration.

- The third tier is a fee of $2,750, to be paid by registrants for whom DDTC has reviewed, adjudicated or issued a response to more than ten applications during the twelve-month period ending 90 days prior to the expiration of their current registration. An additional fee will be determined by multiplying $250 times the number of applications, after the initial ten, for which DDTC has reviewed, adjudicated or issued a response during the twelve-month period ending 90 days prior to the expiration of the current registration.

Number of Applications	Fee
Renewal of or Initial Registration	$2,250
1- 10 Applications following Registration	$2,750
Over 10 Applications following Registration	$2750 + $250 each application after 10.

Fig. 10

After submission of the registration application, plan to wait 3-4 weeks for a response. If approved, the applicant will receive a registration code. **Treasure this code like you do your social security number.** It is a 4-5 character alphanumeric code that will be used for each license application. The first digit will be either an M for manufacturer or a K for broker.

Congratulations! You're registered with DDTC. Now its time to gain access to the service that allows you to apply for a license. The DDTC offers electronic licensing system, known as **D-Trade**, free of charge to registered applicants.

*T*IP! The validity period for registration is one year. The renewal date should be 60 days prior to the expiration to avoid export privileges being revoked.

Submitting applications via the internet is the most expeditious way to submit an application and is highly recommended. In order to gain access, each individual must purchase an Access Certificate for Electronic

Services. Authorized ACES vendors, listed by the DDTC, from whom certificates can be purchased, are IdenTrust and ORC.

Install your digital certificate from one of the approved providers. Follow up with a fax to the DDTC with a letter signed by an empowered official providing the name of the *super user*, as well as other required information explained in more detail on the DDTC website. *Do not miss this step.* Having super user access will allow the applicant to view and track an application status.

After these steps are completed, the registrant should now be able to apply for a license through D-trade.

REFERENCES

Getting Started with Defense Trade

http://www.pmddtc.state.gov/documents/ddtc_getting_started.doc

BIS: SNAP-R

http://www.bis.doc.gov/snap/index.htm

Registration DS-2032

http://www.state.gov/m/a/dir/forms/

Transmittal Letter

http://www.pmddtc.state.gov/registration/registration_transmittal_letter.doc

CHAPTER 5

HOW DO I APPLY FOR A LICENSE UNDER EAR?

This chapter will discuss steps for license application under EAR jurisdiction, utilizing the automated SNAP-R license submission process. (This assumes that it has already been established that the article is controlled and there are no license exceptions).

According to the BIS, most items regulated by the EAR are classified as EAR99 (the catch-all classification indicating that a license is not needed) and less than 5% of all exports require BIS License. This is good news, as applying for a BIS license can be time-consuming (though necessary). However, applying for a license through EAR is significantly easier than going through the ITAR licensing process. Some reasons for this are:

- The chances of needing an export license through the BIS are not high.

- Applying via the internet using SNAP-R is free and no annual fees are involved.

- The EAR has one only type of export license application (the BIS-748B Multipurpose application form found in **Appendix K**).

Let's Begin the Export Licensing Process

It is usually the U.S. Principal Party of Interest (USPPI) that applies for an export license. The USPPI is the person in the U.S. that receives the primary benefit, monetary or otherwise, of the export transaction While the exporter or reexporter of a commodity may apply for a license on their own, they may also delegate an exporter or rexporter to a 3rd party upon submission of Third Party Certification Letter to the BIS.

Through SNAP-R, you may submit an application for:

- Export License
- Reexport
- Commodity Classification Request
- Agriculture license exception notice

Types of License Applications

*T*IP! Applicants may request emergency processing with the Outreach and Education Services Division of the Office of Export Services. The reviewers will use their best judgment to discern if its an emergency so take caution! "I forgot" most likely won't get the application processed faster.

1. Export and Reexport License Application

Utilizing SNAP-R, you'll submit an application for export or reexport electronically (Note: hard copy, i.e. paper, format is no longer accepted). The interface will mirror the format of the BIS-748P Multipurpose Application Form **(See Appendix K)**. The validity period for a export and reexport license is normally two years from date of issuance.

2. Classification Request

Once again, you'll submit through SNAP-R using the Multipurpose Application Form. BIS can provide you with the correct ECCN for up to six items. To assist BIS with classification of the article, provide as much information as possible, such as descriptive literature, brochures, technical specifications, etc.

Be prepared to provide the following information:

- Parties to a transaction, including names and addresses.
- Statement that a power of attorney is on file (if applicable).
- Purchaser.
- Intermediate Consignee.
- Ultimate Consignee.
- ECCN Number.
- Manufacturer.
- Product details such as model number, technical description, quantity to be exported, and unit price.

Supporting Documentation

The EAR requirements for supporting documentation are specified on a case-by-case basis in 748 of EAR . It is your responsibility as applicant to know what type of supporting documents your article requires. In the SNAP-R select the check box(es) that apply to your article and then attach those documents with your application. (Note: All original supporting documentations should be kept on file for 5 years).

Now we'll cover each of the these documents, along with the circumstances under which they should be submitted. For greater detail, review Part 748 of the EAR.

BIS-711/Statement of Ultimate Consignee and/or Purchaser

This document consists of specific statements made by the purchaser or ultimate consignee on a BIS-711, or on the purchaser's or ultimate consignee's letterhead addressing and attesting to certain details of the transaction outlined in 748.11(e) of the EAR.

A BIS-711 must be submitted if:

- The country of ultimate destination is in either Group D:2, D:3, or D:4.

A BIS-711 does not need to be submitted if:

- There is an International Import Certificate, PRC End-user certificate (and further explained in 748.11 (a) (1);
- The applicant same person as ultimate consignee;
- The application is valued under $5,000; or
- The transaction meets the exemptions stated in 748.9.

(See Appendix J for an example of this document).

BIS 647/ End-User Statement/ Import Certificate

An import certificate is normally required if the value of the commodity exceeds $50,000 and the ultimate destination is a country specified in 748.9 (b)(2). At the time of this writing, these countries are:

Argentina	Finland
Australia	France
Austria	Germany
Belgium	Greece
Bulgaria	Hong Kong
China	Hungary
Czech Republic	India

Denmark	Portugal
Japan	Romania
Italy	Singapore
Ireland	Slovakia
Korea	Spain
Liechtenstein	Sweden
Luxembourg	Switzerland
Netherlands	Taiwan
New Zealand	Turkey
Norway	United Kingdom
Pakistan	
Poland	

- The End-User Statement is normally required for all commodities controlled for NS purposes and exceeding $50,000.

- An End-User Statement is required for all licensable transactions going to the PRC for any control reason with a value exceeding $50,000. However there are exceptions to the $50,000 threshold for certain commodities going to the PRC listed in 748.10 (b) (3).

- The End-User Statement is required for an export destined to the PRC with ECCN 6A003 exceeding $5000.

(See Appendix I for an example of this document.)

Letter of Explanation

A letter of explanation describes the facts surrounding an export transaction such as involved parties, commodity, and mode of transport. It is utilized when an export or reexport that has been made without a license authorization. The letter of explanation should also be attached when submitting a license for export or reexport of technology.

Letter of Assurance

The letter of assurance must be completed on company letterhead and contain information assuring BIS that the company will abide by BIS regulations.

BIS 647/ Delivery Verification

The requirement for delivery verification is normally required as a condition to the approved license application. It is possible that a corporation may be requested by a foreign entity to issue a delivery verification. Verifications are issued by the government of the importer's country normally in relationship to products controlled for national security reasons.

(See Appendix H for an example of this document).

Special Comprehensive License (SCL)

T IP!

In 748.9 of the EAR you can find exemptions from documentation submission requirements.

This document option, selectable through Block 5 of the Multipurpose Application, *(Appendix K)* meets the needs of businesses with multiple and continuing exports. In lieu of an individual license for each shipment, this allows the exporter to ship to approved customers. For those aware of this option, the SCL can increase your organization's competitiveness and supply chain speed. All countries are eligible under the SCL except Cuba, Iran, Iraq, North Korea, Sudan and Syria (752). To be approved for SCL, you must:

- Prove mechanisms are in place to ensure compliance with provisions of the EAR.

- Submit a comprehensive narrative on how the proposed export transaction will work (752.6 (c) (4).

- Demonstrate compliance with an Internal Control Program, which is explained in 752.11 of the EAR.

(See Appendix I for an example of this document.)

Deemed Export Application

A deemed export license can be submitted using SNAP-R under the export application choice, or, if applicable, the reexport application choice. As discussed in previous chapters, a deemed export is the release of "controlled" U.S. technology, data or services to a foreign national in or outside the United States. An example of a deemed export is transfer from the United States to France. Deemed Reexport would be the subsequent exchange from France to Italy.

Deemed Exports do not include fundamental research, public information available on patent applications, educational information associated with academic institutions or publicly available technology. Nor does it include those technologies subject to exceptions such as:

- CIV - Civil End-Use
- TSR - Technology and Software Under Restriction
- APP - Applied Peak Performance

As a reminder, a Foreign National is considered anyone who:

- Is NOT a U.S. citizen.
- Is a Foreign National NOT granted U.S. citizenship.
- Does NOT hold permanent residence or green card holder status.

- Is NOT a "protected individual", such as political refugees and political asylum holders further defined in 8 U.S.C 1324b(a)(3).

An applicant is likely to have a deemed export situation if they deal with controlled products, technology, or data and have foreign national employees, interns or students at their U.S. based company. A deemed export may also occur if the company conducts tours or training sessions to foreign nationals pertaining to controlled technology, data or services.

For a deemed export application, the foreign national(s) to whom your company would like to grant access should expect to provide the following in the license application via SNAP-R:

- Foreign National's address in the U.S. and in home country.

- Detailed explanation of the type of technical data and/or services the foreign national will need access to and the ECCN(s).

- Explanation that explains the reason the foreign national requires access to controlled technology

SUPPORTING DOCUMENTATION

Letter of Explanation

Be sure to address the exact location the technology or software will be used. Identify all parties to this transaction and type of technology and availability abroad of comparable foreign technology. Also, identify with which format the release of technology to the foreign national will occur, as well as your internal technology control plan. An internal technology plan explains the mechanism internally in place to control or restrict the release of controlled technology and articles to unauthorized individuals.

- Resume
- Job Description
- Safeguards to restrict access(which may already be in the Technology Control Plan)
- Non-Disclosure Statement

After submitting the application, expect to receive one of the following responses:

- *Approved:* Allows the applicant to proceed with export transaction.

- *Approved with Provisions:* The application has been approved; however, there are written limitations and stipulations for the export.

- *Denied:* Exportation of the article is prohibited.

- *Returned Without Action(RWA):* An application is returned to the applicant with out approval or denial due to incomplete or insufficient information. The issue should be addressed and the Multipurpose application form should be submitted again.

<u>**EXERCISE:**</u>

In general, what is not considered a deemed export?

ANSWER:

Deemed Exports do not include fundamental research, public information available on patent applications, educational information associated with academic institutions or publicly available technology

REFERENCES AND RESOURCES

Export Administration Regulations 15 CFR

Forms provided by Export Administration Regulations
http://www.bis.doc.gov

CHAPTER 6

HOW DO I APPLY FOR A LICENSE UNDER ITAR?

Applying for an export license through the DDTC can be an arduous task, especially for the beginner. The guidelines for license application are not transparent, and often applicants can find themselves confused as to exactly what information is required. Often, an applicant has a customer that needs the merchandise immediately, or a foreign national employee needs immediate access to controlled information in order to do his/her job. This frequent need for immediate shipment or access does not leave most corporations with much time to wait for a license approval. What happens, for example, if an applicant receives the dreaded RWA-Returned Without Action? RWAs occur when an application is submitted to DDTC and it is neither approved or denied, but returned without approval. The RWA normally requests missing or incomplete information that the applicant must supply and resubmit before approval can be granted. In 2006 RWA were estimated to amount to 15% of license applications. Other responses to license applications from the DDTC include:

- *Approved:* Export of the commodity, software or technology is granted.

- *Approved with Provisos:* License is approved with certain conditions and limitations.

- *Denied:* Export of the commodity is prohibited.

Types of License Applications

There are many types of license applications. DDTC issues the following types of licenses:

- DSP-5: Application/License for Permanent Export of Unclassified Defense Articles and Related Unclassified Technical Data.

- DSP-6: Application for Amendment to a DSP-5 License.

- DSP-61: Application/License for Temporary Import of Unclassified Defense Articles.

- DSP-62: Application for Amendment to a DSP-61 License.

- DSP-73: Application/License for Temporary Export of Unclassified Defense Articles.

- DSP-74: Application for Amendment to a DSP-73 License.

- DSP-83: Nontransfer and Use Certificate may be downloaded for official use.

- DSP-85: Application for Permanent/Temporary Export or Temporary Import of Classified Defense Articles and Related Classified Technical Data, can only be submitted in hardcopy.

- DSP-94: Authority to Export Defense Articles Sold under the Foreign Military Sales Program.

- DSP-119: Application for Amendment to License for Export or Temporary Import of Classified or Unclassified Defense Articles and Related Classified Technical Data.

- DS-4071: Export Declaration of Defense Technical Data or Services.

- DS-6000: General Inquiry.

- DS-6001: Advisory Opinion.

- DS-6002: Prior Notification.

- DS-6003: Reconsideration of Unclassified Proviso(s).

- DS-6004: Request to Change End User, End Use, and/or Destination of Hardware.

The scope of this book does not allow time to cover each license application. There are three license applications most frequently used by organizations, DSP-5, DSP-61 and DSP-73.

DSP-5: Hardware

Many exporters find the hardest part of the application process is not filling out the license application itself, but in providing the proper supporting documentation, so the DDTC wont issue an RWA, Normally on the RWA, it "vaguely" states the reason why the license application has been rejected, but you will often be left guessing. Applicants must make the stated corrections and resubmit, *referencing the RWA number from the previously rejected application. (See Appendix C for a sample of the DSP-5 form).*

Neither the DDTC nor its guidelines instruct you with certainty on the type of supporting documentation that should accompany a license application. In fact, when electronically filing for a license, you will be given the options listed below, and it is up to you to decipher which options apply to your circumstances.

- Purchase Document: The PO should be addressed to you from the foreign company on letterhead, date, type of commodity, quantity, unit price, and total price. If the end-user is not stated on the purchase document a separate letter stating the end-user of the product sometimes referred to as a letter of intent.

- Descriptive literature and/or technical data.

- Letter of explanation. This should only be submitted when the information cannot be included in the application form or attachment and is necessary to add to the contents of the submission.

- Form DSP-83, Non-transfer and Use Certificate, when applicable. You must retain the signed original and make it available to PM/DDTC, upon request.

Not all of these supporting documents are required; it depends on the your circumstances. For instance, if you are exporting a product that is in "furtherance of an agreement," such as a TAA and MLA, you must submit a transmittal letter and supporting documentation, i.e. copies of the agreement/ amendments and pertinent sections which relate to and authorize exports of hardware, and/or the letter of explanation by agreement holder of relevant document. Only the agreement holder or U.S. signatory may obtain a license in furtherance of an agreement.. In addition, the value of the hardware should be identified. It is up to you to make an educated guess dependant upon the product or data, end-use and end-user that will determine the type of documentation that should travel with the license application.

SUPPORTING DOCUMENTATION

The following are suggestions on the type of documentation that should accompany the DSP-5. Unfortunately, there is no guarantee these documents will be sufficient, because approval also depends on the reviewer of the application and of course the specific product, data or software.

At minimum you should provide:

- **Eligibility letter:** This document should accompany most applications. In brief, it is a letter signed by the empowered official of the company attesting that neither he/she, nor any of the executive officers, have violated criminal statutes, and the individual to the best of his or her knowledge is a citizen of the United States.

  To read more about letter and its contents, go to 126.13 of the ITAR regulations. Please see Appendix G for sample eligibility letter provided by the Department of State.

- **Purchase Order (PO) or Proforma Invoice:** Take care that the PO amount matches exactly the amount entered in Block 12 of the application. Recent requirements by the DDTC further require the PO or letter of intent be addressed to the U.S. party registered with the DDTC, submitting the application as well as selling the defense articles. The purchase document should also reflect the ultimate end-use and end-user of the article with an issue date that does not exceed more than a year from date of application.

- **Letter of Intent/Transmittal Letter:** This letter from the foreign buyer must be written on company letterhead, stating the end-use such as repair, overhaul, modification, upgrade, etc.

Recent additions added by the DDTC may also require a copy of the signed contract to check the legitimacy of the transaction.

While you will have space to describe the article, if the article is considered significant military equipment (SME), providing more descriptive literature is suggested. Providing descriptive literate, brochures, technical data/drawings in general is a good idea

Optional supporting documents include the **DSP-83** (Non-Transfer Certificate). This document is only required if the article is considered significant military equipment

(SME). Articles qualifying as SME are defined in 120.7 of the ITAR, and are considered articles with the capacity for substantial military utility or capability. This certificate essentially makes the foreign end-user promise that they won't reexport or resell the licensable article.

If this applies, don't forget to check the box in Block 11 of the application.

At some point in time, you may make a mistake on a license or circumstances may change, which will necessitate a change to the license afterapplication has been approved. The DDTC only allows you to make certain changes "amendments" to an application. Changes may only be made to:

- Add a freight forwarder or U.S. consignor.
- Correct a typographical error.
- Change a source or manufacturer of the commodity.
- Change a part number of exported item.
- Change a location of applicant or subsidiary.
- Change a license due to acquisition or merger.

DSP-5 FOR FOREIGN NATIONAL

Title VII (42 USC 2000e-2(g)): provides an exception to unlawful employment practices, which allows an employer to refuse to employ a foreign person if the duties to be performed are in the interest of the national security of the United States.

(g) National security

Notwithstanding any other provision of this subchapter, it shall not be an unlawful employment practice for an employer to fail or refuse to hire and employ any individual for any position, for an employer to discharge any individual from any position, or for an employment agency to fail or refuse to refer any individual for employment in any position, or for a labor organization to fail or refuse to refer any individual for employment in any position, if—

(1) the occupancy of such position, or access to the premises in or upon which any part of the duties of such position is performed or is to be performed, is subject to any requirement imposed in the interest of the national security of the United States under any security program in effect pursuant to or administered under any statute of the United States or any Executive order of the President; and

(2) such individual has not fulfilled or has ceased to fulfill that requirement.

However, foreign persons can contribute valuable skills and knowledge to a U.S. company, and may be worth hiring. If a company is going to engage in hiring a foreign person it is highly suggested the Human Resources departments takes on the following practices at a minimum.

> **T**IP! Are you having foreign nationals visit a location where they will view and/or hear technical information about a controlled product? If they are Canadian, you may apply for a Canadian exemption in ITAR section 126.5 as well as exemptions for plant visits in 125.5.

- Screening the foreign person against all restricted parties and the country list.

- Establishing a system to determine if the foreign individual's position requires access to controlled articles, or data. If so, a DSP-5 must be applied for and, until approval is granted, access to such articles and technology must be restricted.

Before proceeding with the application process, first establish whether or not the employee making application is a foreign national by U.S. Department of State standards. According to the Department of State, a foreign national is anyone who is not a U.S. citizen, permanent resident of the U.S. or is a "protected person" such as a refugee. If they fall under this group and will have access to controlled data or service, a DSP-5 must be applied.

A DSP-5 is used commodities as well as for "deemed exports". It is defined as the release of articles, technology or source code subject to the ITAR. Providing controlled technology to a non-U.S. citizen in the U.S. is considered an export like any other physical export to another country. If an applicant employs foreign nationals who will need to receive controlled information or controlled technology while on the job, they should apply with the State Department prior to receiving access to this information. The underlying purpose of this regulation is to stop controlled U.S. technology and articles from getting into the wrong hands.

With a few exceptions, a DSP-5 application should be filled out as usual. Review Guidelines for Licensing of Foreign Nationals in the United States, at the Directorate of Defense Trade Controls website.

Tips for completing a DSP-5 Foreign National:

Block 3: Country of Ultimate Destination should be the country identified on the employee's passport.

Block 10: Commodity: State the technical data that will be provided by applicant to the foreign national employee.

Block 14: Foreign End-User: State the employee's residence in home country or where he intends to return.

Block 18: Name and Address of Foreign Intermediate Foreign Consignee. If applicable, list the country/countries in which the employee maintains residency.

Block 19: Name and Address of Consignor in the United States. If the employee is already in the U.S., state the address.

Block 20: Specific Purpose for which Material is Required: Explain in detail specific information and technical data the employee will need access to in order to perform his or her job. Have their job description handy to support this statement up with specifics of their job functions.

Suggested supporting documentation for a DSP-5 Foreign National Application includes:

1. Cover letter explaining the requirement and scope of the foreign national's employment This document may also provide information about the company, items that are not controlled and those that are controlled, as well as the data or products that will be accessed by a foreign national employee in order to carry out the assigned duties as described in job announcement.

   Important: Even though this will be explained in Box 20 on the DSP-5, this is a good opportunity to further clarify exactly what technical data the foreign national will be exposed to and access.

2. Copy of the individual's passport and work authorization Department of Homeland Security, U.S. Citizenship and Immigration Services, (when residing in the U.S.).

3. Resume supporting the foreign national's claims to expertise in the field qualifying them for duties involving access to the technical data in question.

4. Job Description.

5. Detailed description of technical data to be. released and copies of technical data as necessary.

6. Non Disclosure Agreement.

7. Technology Control Plan: This is a plan your company creates explaining what mechanisms are in place to safeguard its controlled technologies from unauthorized users. The plan normally includes an expression of the corporation's commitment to export compliance, the type of physical security in place at the facility, information security, personnel screening procedures, etc.

DSP-61 and DSP-73 – Temporary Import and Export

A DSP-61 is used for temporary **import** of unclassified defense articles and a DSP-73 is for temporary **export** of unclassified defense articles. Conditions for temporary import/export licenses include the return of the articles within a 4-year period, and a prohibition on transfer of title on the defense article that has benn temporarily imported or exported. (*See Appendix D and E for samples of DSP-61 and DSP-73*)

*T*IP! A DSP-61 or DSP-73 cannot be used for temporary import or export of technical data. Any export of technical data is considered a permanent export.

Supporting documentation options for applications DSP-61 and DSP-73 include:

- Firearms and Ammunitions Import Permit.
- Firearms and Ammunitions Letter of Explanation.
- Other amplifying data. (e.g. briefing , proposal)
- Precedent (identical/similar cases).
- Product brochures.
- Supplementary explanation of transaction (white paper).
- Technical drawings, schematics, or blue prints.
- Transaction exception request.
- ITAR 126.13 Eligibility Letter.

Suggested supporting documentation:

At one point, these types of license applications rarely required supporting documentation. Now, applicants should almost always include an Eligibility Letter. (*See Appendix G for a sample*).

In the case of temporary import/export for the purpose of overhaul, repair, modifications, or upgrades, a Transmittal Letter is required. This is a letter explaining the need for the temporary export or import and identifying roles of each party listed to the license. In the case of a DSP-61 (temporary import) the transmittal letter must be from the foreign owner of the defense articles requesting the transaction. For a DSP-73 (temporary export) the transmittal letter should be from the U.S. applicant explaining the need for the temporary export and the roles of each party to the license.

*T*IP! When resubmitting an application that has been returned without action (RWA), be sure to reference the RWA number. Reviewers may get upset if the RWA number is consistently omitted and refer application to the compliance department.

If the applicant is temporarily importing or exporting firearms, submit an Import Permit from the foreign government and Letter of Explanation describing why the firearms have to be temporarily imported or exported.

If the article falls under SME category of Significant Military Equipment, a DSP-83/Non-transfer and User Certificate must accompany the application.

As a reminder, if the temporary import or export is in "furtherance of an agreement" (such as a TAA or MLA) the agreement should be referenced and additional supporting documenation should be attached.

For more details on specific supporting documentation, visit http://pmddtc.state.gov/docs/AG_Section_9.4_Replacement.doc.

EXERCISE:

Company A needs to export an article to their foreign subsidiary in Italy for repair. There is no attached Agreement i.e. TAA, MLA or WDA.

What type of license application is needed and what type of supporting documents should Company A submit in support of the application?

ANSWER:

Completed DSP-73 with Eligibility Letter, Transmittal Letter from the U.S. applicant

REFERENCES AND RESOURCES

International Traffic and Arms Regulations (22 CFR)

Export Administration Regulations (15 CFR)

Guidelines for Preparing DSP-5, DSP-61. and DSP-73
http://www.pmddtc.state.gov/sl_dtrade.htm

Department of State form DSP-5, DSP-61, DSP-73, DSP-83 referenced in the International Traffic in Arms

Regulations copies of forms available from the Department of State's Directorate of Defense Trade Controls (DDTC)

*Sample Technology Control Plan provided by DDTC **(See Appendix F)***

Sample Eligibility Letter provided by DDTC

CHAPTER 7

FORMULATING AGREEMENTS

Part 125. 4(b) (2) of ITAR specifies various exemptions that apply to exports of technical data, which requireapproval from the DDTC. As opposed to submitting a license application such as a DSP-5 or a DSP61 the applicant for an exchange of technical data, services and/or related hardware must submit a Manufacturing License Agreement (MLA) or a Technical Assistance Agreement (TAA) for approval by the DDTC. *(See Appendix M for a Sample TAA/MAA.)*

A **Technical Assistance Agreement (TAA)** is an agreement for the performance of defense services by, and/or the disclosure of technical data to, overseas companies and/or individuals, which is necessary for said foreign corporation or entity to perform a specific project through discussion and exchange of technical data. If specified within a TAA, export hardware may also be approved to be sent to agreed-upon foreign parties. The action of exporting hardware or technical data specified in a TAA is termed as 'in furtherance of an agreement." (See ITAR 124.3 (a) for further explanation of the "furtherance of an agreement" concept.

According to ITAR 120.21, a **Manufacturing License Agreement (MLA)** is an agreement that allows a U.S. person to grant a foreign person authorization to manufacture defense articles abroad.

This may involve the export of technical data or defense services to the foreign persons in order to manufacture the commodities. (There is also a Warehouse and Distribution Agreement (WDA), which is an agreement to establish a warehouse or distribution center abroad for defense article to be exported to the United States and later to be distributed to approved sales areas. This chapter will not touch upon this type of agreement but for those interested, more information can be found in ITAR 120.23.)

A **defense service** is defined by ITAR 120.9 as the furnishing of assistance (including training) to foreign persons, whether in the United States or abroad in the design, development, engineering, manufacture, production, assembly, testing, repair, maintenance, modification, operation, demilitarization, destruction, processing or use of defense articles. It also includes providing foreign persons any controlled technical data, whether in the U.S. or abroad. (A defense service includes military training of foreign units and forces.)

Providing defense services and technical data to foreign nationals or foreign units is commonly called a deemed export". The transfer to **any** foreign national of **any** controlled technology, even if the applicant is physically in the U.S. at the time of transmission, is considered an export to that foreign national's home country. This concept can be a difficult one to understand and for a corporation to control, because its transmission is not a tangible product, but rather intangible information and/or communications. However, a deemed export needs prior approval in the form of a license from the applicable agency . Previously, applicants who employed a foreign person were required to submit a TAA and DSP-5 application. The DDTC recently recognized this as double licensing and (in their words) redundant.

Therefore, only a DSP-5 (for unclassified data, services or articles) or a DSP-85 (for classified data, service, or articles), are required to authorize the employment of a foreign person, and which additionally allows them a certain level of access to technical data and services of their employer **only**. This chapter will explain how to apply for such a license when it is controlled under the USML.

APPLYING WITH A TAA

Formulating a TAA (ITAR 120.22) is just one step in the application process to get approval for the exchange of controlled technical information and/or services. The review and adjudication of an agreement application should take 60 days from date of receipt, and an agreement approved by the office of Defense Trade Controls Licensing (DTCL) will not exceed ten years in duration. An application for TAA and/or MLA must be sent to the Directorate of Defense by courier, mail or in person. For new agreements not requiring congressional notification, applicants should submit one original and seven collated copies to the DDTC. The following documents should be included in the submission package. (***Please see Appendice L for a sample.***)

1. <u>TRANSMITTAL LETTER</u>

A transmittal letter is an explanatory letter that provides an executive summary of the agreement being submitted. Part 124.12 of ITAR requires certain information be included in the content of the letter such as:

- Applicant's Registration Number
- Contract number or proposal number, if derived from a U.S. government contract or bid.
- Military Security Classification of the data.
- Any applicable patent applications that disclose the subject matter of equipment or data.
- A statement of the value of the actual or estimated value of the agreement, including any articles that will be exported in furtherance of the agreement. Value does not necessarily mean the amount payable, it is the estimated value of the agreement.

Here's the breakdown of valuation definitions:

- **Value of Hardware**: This is the value at time of export and is not the value after incorpation into the manufactured end item.

- **Defense Services**: This is the cost of manpower incurred by the U.S. company.

- **Technical data**: This is the value assigned to the technical data that will be transferred to a foreign party.

- Statement indicating whether there are any foreign military sales credits or loan guarantees involved in the financing of this agreement.

- Describe any classified information involved.

*T*IP! Making sure to keep track of hardware that is exported in connection to a TAA and notate it on your DSP-5/7, ensuring you do not go over the value of the exports specified in the TAA. In block 23 or 21, specify "the hardware was originally exported under (agreement number)". If there is a need to increase the value of hardware exports, amendments to the TAA may be applied for to the DDTC. It is worth looking at ITAR 123.16 (b) (1-5) for certain exemptions from having to apply for licenses (such as DSP-5) regarding permanent export of unclassified hardware specified in your TAA, MLA, etc.

For data that is considered classified, section 124.12(9) explains additional details an applicant must include in the transmittal letter.

2. ELIGIBILITY/CERTIFICATION LETTER (126.13)

The Eligibility Letter accompanies applications for license

and agreements and must be signed by an empowered official. It ensures that you abide by the provisions in section 120.25. Most of the letter is a certification that no individuals in high positions within the company, such as the CEO, or President, have been convicted of violating any U.S. criminal laws specified in 120.27. *(Please refer to the Eligibility/Certification Letter Sample in Appendix G).*

3. PROPOSED TECHNICAL ASSISTANCE AGREEMENT

The proposed agreement for a TAA sets forth each individual's role, scope and nature of the technical data to be exported, as well as the type of venue in which it will be exchanged (i.e. by email, fax, phone etc.). When reviewing the **attached TAA Template (See Appendix M)** provided by the DDTC, Part I. ITAR 124.7 the TAA can be sequentially broken up into the following:

- **General Purpose of Agreement:** Describe the parties to the agreement and brief summary of technical assistance to be provided.

- **Article I (124.7: Statement of Services and Shared Technical Assistance and Data:** describe in detail the kind of data and know-how to be exchanged. Ensure the body of this text contains all the information specified n 124.7 (1-4). Under 124.7(1), describe in detail the defense article and related technical data and services. Under 124.7(2), further describe technical data and services and any manufacturing know-how that may be provided by your company to the foreign company. Under 124.7(3), specify the duration of the agreement, which may not exceed ten years and must be in the formation of day, month and year. Under 124.7(4), identify countries where manufacturing, production or other form of transfer may occur.

- **TAA Sample Article I, Part (c)** allows you to authorize or not authorize dual/third country nationals, access to data, services or articles. "Third Country" refers to a person that has nationalities in a country or countries other than the country of the foreign signatory of the agreement. "Dual national" is a person that holds nationality from one or more countries outside of the country of the foreign signatory of the agreeement.

- **Article II U.S. Department of State Required Clauses (124.8):** To parahrase, these required clauses are important because they bind the signatories to:

  - Not amend the license without approval;

  - Agree to U.S. laws and regulations;

  - Not interference with any contract or subcontract between the U.S. Government and the signatories;

  - Recognize that the U.S. Government is not liable for any infringements to patent or proprietary rights of the signatories;

  - Agree that technical data, services and articles specified in the agreement are strictly intended for those parties, and that no transfer to third countries or nationals is allowed.

  - Recognize that even after the termination of this agreement certain articles referring to the U.S. Government still apply.

- **Agreement of Signatures done after approval of Department of State.** One agreement of signed agreement must be submitted to DTCL no later than 30 days after it enters into force (124.4.(a).

The TAA template, found in **Appendix M**, suggests the applicant follow the formatting precisely, and add or omit parts that do not fit the applicant's particular situation. For instance, in many TAA's (including the sample), there is a section that requires an attachment of a Non-Disclosure Agreement to be signed by the involved foreign party.

However, if you are doing business with a company or nationals of NATO countries, section 124.16 of the ITAR does not require a signature. The purpose of the Non-Disclosure agreement is to get a written agreement from the signatory foreign individual(s) that the transfer of data or services outside of the U.S. to any foreign entity not covered by the TAA is prohibited.

Normally, as an Appendix to the TAA, applicants will go into greater depth about the type of service or technical information they are to exchange in what is called a "Scope of Work". This information is not required, but highly suggested.

APPLYING WITH A MLA

The MLA grants a foreign person the right to manufacture or assemble U.S. defense articles abroad. Presumably, in order to manufacture the product outside of the U.S., the foreign entity will need the know how to manufacture the goods. This could require the exchange/export technical data or possibly the performance of a defense service in order to manufacture the commodity. You will need to collate basically the same package as a TAA.

Some of the similarities and difference between the TAA process and MLA process include:

- **MLA Only:** Prior approval or notification to the DDTC is needed for the sale or manufacture abroad of significant military equipment. Requires clauses in 124.9 of the ITAR be included in the proposed agreement, verbatim. One of main clauses specifies that no export, sale, transfer or other disposition of the licensed article to any country outside of approved countries and/or individuals specified in the MLA.

- **TAA and MLA:** 22 CFR 124.8 provides the required clauses to put in both proposed agreements. The clauses must be stated verbatim and any modifications of these clauses will result in disapproval of the request. To parahrase, these required clauses are important because they bind the signatories to the stipulations found on the previous page. The Non Transfer and Use Form (DSP-83) is required for both types of agreements when significant military equipment or classified articles are involved.

In all these documents (with exception of the Certification Letter), the applicant will be addressing the man-ufacturing know-how that will be furnished to foreign individuals as well as:

> *T*IP! Try to make the scope of a TAA as broad as possible. For instance: as opposed to specifying exact names of each individual requiring access to technical data, try mentioning the corporation and the nationalities of those needing access to technical data. This will allow for flexibility and save time in the case of employee turnover.

- Any manufacturing rights.

- The commodity to be manufactured.

- The type of data that will be exchanged as a result of manufacturing in this country.

- The countries where the manufacturing, production, processing or sale will take place and the duration.

Congressional Notification

Even though Congress is kept aware of approved and denied licenses by the Department of State and Department of Commerce, there are instances when Congress wants to know about the granting of any license pertaining to exports of defense articles and services of any major defense equipment as defined in ITAR 120.8, and they want to know prior to approval. This means that if a TAA or MLA involves the manufacture or technical transfer of a major defense article, Congressional notification is required. Two types of Congressional notification specified in Section 36 of the Arms Export Control Act is notification of value and notification of manufacture of significant military equipment (SME) abroad. Examples include:

- Major defense equipment sold under a contract in the amount $14 million or more or defense article of services sold under contract to any country that is not a NATO member in the amount of $50 million or more.

- Major defense equipment for NATO members and Japan, Australia, New Zealand or South Korea sold under a contract of of major defense equipment of 25 million or more or defense articles or services valued at 100 million or more.

- Firearms controlled under Category I of USML in the amount of $1 million or more.

Part 123.15 of the ITAR further explains other stipulations. Therefore, if your MLA or TAA involves a major defense article in the value computation within the transmittal letter and MLA/TAA itself, you should add Congressional Notification Value, that is the value of the contract for such articles.

After compiling all this information and documents you are now finished. Now its time to submit a package. A submission package refers to Letter of Transmittal, Certification Letter and Proposed Agreeement or Amendment. If you have ever bought and closed on a house, you'll appreciate the relationship both have in terms of the amount of paperwork one must copy.

- New and Amended Agreements: An original plus 7 collated copies of agreement package

- New and Amended Agreement requiring Congressional notification or Highly Sensitive

Commodities of Countries: An original plus 9 collated copies of agreement package.

Technical Data and Defense Services	$1,000,000
Hardware Permanent Export by DSP-5 or DSP-85 Temporary Export by DSP-73 or DSP-85 Temporary Import by DSP-61 or DSP-85 Total Hardware Total Hardware for Notification	 $98,000,000 $1,000,000 $500,000 $99,500,000 $98,000,000
Total Value of the Agreement	$100,500,000
Congressional Notification Value (Total Articles and Services Sold Under a Contract)	$99,000,000

Fig 10

When an exporter undertakes the TAA/MLA process for the first time, the DDTC provides a helpful publication entitled "Guidelines for Preparing Agreements".

Legal counsel or an export consultant can also assist with the technical legal language of these agreements to ensure that all individuals, processes and data are being adequately covered.

References and Resources

Guidelines for Preparing Agreements: Technical Assistance Agreements, Manufacturing License Agreements and Warehouse and Distribution Agreements provided by DDTC at http://www.pmddtc.state.gov/docs/agbook.pdf)

CHAPTER 8

AUTOMATED EXPORT SYSTEM

The Automated Export System (AES) is an export information gathering and processing system, developed as a joint venture between U.S. Customs and Border Protection, the Bureau of the Census, other Federal agencies. In short, AES is an electronic form of filing a Shipper's Export Declaration (SED). The SED contains information regarding the export transaction, including parties to a transaction, date of exportation of the shipment, consignees and agents for the shipment, Schedule B classifications, and weight and value of the goods. Until recently, exporters had the option of filing the paper copy of the SED Commerce Form 7525-V or filing electronically through the Automated Export System (AES). Now, all of the information must be filed via AES.

AESDirect and AESPcLink are both software systems that are offered by the U.S. Census Bureau, free of charge. AESDirect is the web-based filing option that is available at www.aesdirect.gov. AESPcLink is the stand-alone software version of AESDirect that is available for download from the AESDirect website.

AES Requirements

AES filing is required for export of goods and/or mass-market software valued at more than $2,500 per commodity(s) with the same Schedule B number when shipped:

- From the U.S. to foreign countries, including FTZ located therein.
- From the U.S. to foreign countries including Puerto Rico.
- From Puerto Rico to foreign countries.
- From Puerto Rico to the U.S. Virgin Islands.
- From the U.S. to the U.S. Virgin Islands.

In addition to the list above, the EAR contains these additional requirements.

- All exports subject to the EAR destined to a country in Group E:1 regardless of value must submit data through AES.
- All items shipped out under Validated End-User require AES filing.

Individuals responsible for filing an SED through AES are either the U.S. Principal Party of Interest (USPPI) or authorized U.S. Agent. The USPPI is the person/corporation in the United States that receives the primary benefit monetary or otherwise of the export transaction.

Generally, the USPPI can be the:

- U.S. Seller (wholesaler/distributor) of the merchandise for export.
- U.S. Manufacturer, if selling the merchandise for export.
- U.S. Order Party - Party who directly negotiated between the U.S. seller and foreign buyer and received the order for the export of the merchandise.
- Foreign Entity, if in the U.S. when items are purchased or obtained for export.

The USPPI may file an SED through AES:

- On their own behalf.
- Through a U.S. agent authorized to file on their behalf, such as a freight forwarder, customs broker.
- On behalf of Foreign Principal Party in Interest (FPPI).

The USPPI may elect an authorized U.S. agent to file AES records on their behalf. A freight forwarder or other agent may be designed to complete the AES on the exporter's behalf by giving written consent or a power of attorney.

AES Preparation

The information required to complete the SED via AES includes:

1. Date of exportation.
2. Port of exportation.
3. Ultimate consignee.
4. Intermediate consignee.
5. Forwarding or other agent name and address.
6. Country of ultimate destination.
7. Loading pier.
8. Method of transportation.
9. Exporting carrier.
10. Port of unloading.
11. Containerized.
12. Weight.
13. ECCN.
14. License Authority.
15. Signature in the certification block.

For tracking purposes, AES requires the use of external or internal transaction numbers. The External Transaction Number (XTN) is generated at the time of AES filing by the registered applicant/exporter or agent. The Internal Transaction Number (ITN) is generated by AES after verification of successful completion all information fields and requirements and returned to the filer electronically. The ITN is proof of successful submission and resembles the below:

X20060420000001

What does AES filing have to do with U.S. export controls? AES filing is an important element to complying with U.S. export controls, because filing is required for licensable commodities as well as commodities with license exemptions, irrespective of value for in accordance with both the EAR and ITAR. **Exporting a controlled item under the EAR/ITAR requires AES filing.**

The Department of State has set its own timelines for reporting exports of USML articles, to ensure enough time for the shipment(s) to be properly monitored by CBP prior to the export. The timelines for providing export information to CBP using AES are:

- Air or truck shipments must be electronically filed at least 8 hours prior to departure.
- Sea or rail shipments must be electronically filed at least 24 hours prior to departure.

In general, two options direct the period for submission of export information to AES for commercial commodities. **Option 1** requires all information required for exports to AES prior to exportation. **Option 2** takes into account that an exporter does not always know all the required AES information prior to export. Therefore, Option 2 requires no information prior to exportation for approved USPPI's. However, for commodities requiring a license, approval is needed from the licensing agency to take advantage of this option. Under option 2, the filer must submit information as soon as it is known but no later than 10 working days from date of export.

Exporters are not always able to meet the required filing deadlines. As a result, an emergency shipment procedure is being implemented. The procedure covers emergency shipments of hardware against a valid license if the ultimate destination and end user identified on the license is a government. The deadlines for filing of emergency shipments are:

- Export by truck, least one hour prior to departure from the U.S.

- Export by air at least two hours before any departure from the U.S.

AES participants should keep copies of export documentation readily available for inspection by Customs and Border Protection Inspectors. Electronic transmission of AES are considered export documents and therefore record of such must be kept for 5 years and any false statement made on AES is considered a violation.

In 2008, BIS reported on the top compliance issues they encounter with individuals reporting exports via AES. Be on the look out so you do not repeat these mistakes!

1. Incorrect Use of "No License Required" (NLR).

2. Missing Export Control Classification Number (ECCN).

3. Incorrect Use of EAR99.

4. Invalid Country Use with Commerce Control List(CCL)-Based-Based License Exception.

5. CCL-based license exception not applicable to ECCN.

6. Country mismatch between license and AES destinations.

EXERCISE:

How long prior to export does USPPI have to file AES record for a commodity controlled under the USML and shipped by air?

ANSWER:

8 hours prior to departure.

REFERENCES

AES Direct: http://www.aesdirect.gov

15 CFR Part 30 Foreign Trade Statistics

AES Newsletter January 2009 Issue 34

CHAPTER 9

END-USER SCREENING:

One of the most important aspects of compliance with ITAR/EAR requirements is ensuring that the product, technology or software does not go to prohibited end-users. Therefore, customer screening is an important element in complying with U.S. export controls. There is a common misconception that this screening needs only be conducted for non-U.S. customers. However, this screening should be conducted for all customers and parties to a transaction, such as the person you ship to, sell to, bill to, the freight forwarder, and any others. Screening should be done on a case-by-case basis, ideally before money is exchanged or a contractual agreement is signed. To assist the trade community in detecting customers that may be potential violators, the Department of Commerce publishes a list containing the "Red Flag Indicators".

Red Flag Indicators Checklist

- The customer (or the address) is similar to one of the parties/addresses found on the Commerce Department's (BIS's) list of denied persons.

- The customer or purchasing agent is reluctant to offer information about the end-use of the item.

- The product's capabilities do not fit the buyer's line of business, such as an order for sophisticated computers for a small bakery.

- The item ordered is incompatible with the technical level of the country to which it is being shipped, such as semiconductor manufacturing equipment being shipped to a country that has no electronics industry.

- The customer is willing to pay cash for a very expensive item when the terms of sale would normally call for financing.

- The customer has little or no business background.

- The customer is unfamiliar with the product's performance characteristics but still wants the product.

- Routine installation, training, or maintenance services are declined by the customer.

- Delivery dates are vague, or deliveries are planned for out of the way destinations.

- A freight-forwarding firm is listed as the product's final destination.

- The shipping route is abnormal for the product and destination.

- Packaging is inconsistent with the stated method of shipment or destination.

- When questioned, the buyer is evasive and especially unclear about whether the purchased product is for domestic use, for export, or for reexport.

End-user screening is based on the founding principals behind U.S. export controls. These principals include protecting the national security of the U.S. by ensuring that controlled products, services and technology do not get in the wrong hands. Of top concern is the possibility that certain items could be used for nuclear, missile, chemical and or biological end-uses. Second, is they could be used at the detriment of American economic vitality and technological advantage.

The Office of Foreign Assets Control (OFAC) within the U.S. Treasury department administers all U.S. economic sanctions programs. OFAC monitors compliance with the sanction regulations it administers. Economic sanctions can include prohibitions on import or export of commodities or services including financial services on one or more countries. All U.S. persons are required to abide by U.S. sanctions and embargoes. This includes:

- U.S. citizens in the United States.

- U.S. citizens and permanent residents in and outside the United States.

- Global activities of companies that are organized under U.S. law.

- U.S. companies and offices.

End-user screening is the process of checking the customer against various international lists. The Office of Foreign Assets Control (OFAC) requires screening prior to shipping. The lists of entities or countries vary. They change as political climates change, and as more entities supporting or leading terrorism are discovered. For example, prior to the civil war in 2002, the Ivory Coast was not on the restricted list; however, as regional instability persisted, the country was added and remains on the list today. Since the various lists are not static, the screener should check on a transaction-by-transaction basis.

Shipping an article to a country or entity on these lists can cause the exporter to pay costly penalties. OFAC violations include up to 10 years imprisonment, up to 1 million in corporate fines per violation and up to $100,000 in individual fines per violation. Therefore, apart from the licensing process, knowing and screening the customer is the critical step. If the product or technology falls under the USML, the end-user should check the following lists:

ITAR Denied Party Screening Lists

- Department of Commerce Denied Persons (BIS).
- Department of Commerce Entity List (BIS).
- Department of Commerce "Unverified" List (BIS).
- Department of Commerce "Unverified List" (BIS).
- Department of Treasury Specially Designated Nationals and Blocked Persons (OFAC).
- Department of Treasury Specially Designated Nationals and Blocked Persons (OFAC).
- Department of Treasury Specially Designated Terrorist Organizations and Individuals (OFAC).
- Department of Treasury Specially Designated Narcotic Traffickers and Narcotics Kingpins (OFAC).
- Department of State Terrorist Exclusion List (TEL).
- U.S. Federal Register General Orders.
- Department of State Arms Export control Act Debarred Parties.
- Department of State International Traffic in Arms Regulations Munitions Export Control Orders.
- Department of State Nonproliferation Orders.
- Embargo Countries published on the Federal Register.

Current countries listed are: Afghanistan Burma, Belarus, China (PR), Ivory Coast, Cuba, Cyprus, Democratic Republic of Congo, Eritrea, Haiti, Iran, Iraq, Lebanon, Liberia, Libya, North Korea, Rwanda, Sierra Leone, Somalia, Sri Lanka, Sudan, Syria, Venezuela, Vietnam, Yemen, Zimbabwe.

EAR Denied Party Screening Lists:

- Include ITAR Denied Part List with the exception

of Department of State International Traffic in Arms Regulations Munitions Export control Orders.

• Denied Persons List.

• Unverified List.

• Nonproliferation Sanctions.

• General Order 3 to Part 736.

Another useful tool when conducting an end-user screening is utilizing an End-User Questionnaire/Certificate for those involved in the transaction. Creating or adding questions that may be specific to your industry will increase the effectiveness of the screening.

> *T*IP! Consider acquiring Global Trade software that offers Denied Trade Screening Software. IntegrationPoint.net offers screening software that encompasses all the required lists and a few extras. Included is the automatic saving of export screening results that can meet the due diligence requirements of the Department of State, Commerce and other agencies.

Destination Control Statement

Prior to exporting, you must include a statement on the bill of lading and the invoice informing the recipient that the commodity they are receiving is controlled and is subject to U.S. export control regulations. This gives the customer fair warning that if they re-export the article, data or software contrary to U.S. regulations, it will be considered a violation and civil and criminal penalties may incur. It is prudent for the exporter of the controlled commodity to keep record of this warning to support their compliance in the event an illegal reexport occurs. While the EAR only requires a Destination Control Statement on controlled articles, exporters should consider including this statement for all exports.

The Destination Control Statement for EAR controlled commodities reads as follows:

> *"These commodities, technology or software were exported from the United States in accordance with Export Administration Regulations. Diversion contrary to U.S. law is prohibited."*

The Destination Control Statement for ITAR controlled commodities reads as follows (22 CFR 123.9):

> *"These commodities are authorized by the U.S. Government for export only to (country of ultimate destination) for use by (end-user). They may not be transferred, transshipped, on a non-continuous voyage, or otherwise be disposed of in any other country, either in their original form or after being incorporated into other end-items, without the prior written approval of the U.S. Department of State."*

References and Resources

Export Administration Regulations (EAR)

International Traffic and Arms Regulations (ITAR)

IntegrationPoint.net - Global Trade Software

Bureau of Industry & Security
http://www.bis.doc.gov/enforcement/redflags.htm

CHAPTER 10

COMPLIANCE

It is important that individuals, corporations and institutions involved in exporting controlled commodities have a system in place to ensure compliance. This is typically referred to as an Export Management System (EMS). It also serves as a mitigating factor if a corporation is found to have violated export controls, by showing that offense was not done intentionally. This system should encourage the exporter to DO the following.

General Compliance

DO adhere to the license quantity and value limits, and any other conditions when granted license approval. Also, make sure you can identify and track all ITAR controlled items and technical data. Identification of ITAR articles can be done in various ways, such as tagging and physical segregation of ITAR articles from non-controlled commercial items, etc. In the event of temporary exports, the ability to track the shipment date and return date is also critical since there is a specified time limit for the return of the article.

DO have a compliance procedure that addresses the handling of suspected violations and encourages employees to report any concerns. The exporting of licensable goods to countries or foreign nationals requires a structured corporate compliance program. This is important not only to show "due diligence" to the Department of Commerce or

Department of State but also to create corporate transparency in the handling of licensable articles.

DO have a corporate export administration organization chart and description such as flow charts of company defense trade functions.

DO have procedures for re-export/retransfers to foreign person(s) within or outside the U.S for end-use not included in State department authorization.

DO include a Destination Control Statement on company invoices, bills of lading, air waybills or other types of visible export documents, as required by EAR 758.6 and 123.9 (b) of ITAR. This statement makes the purchaser aware that if they subsequently decide to ship or sell the product internationally, even after its release from the seller's custody, it is still bound by the laws and regulations of the EAR or ITAR.

DO enlist upper management. A commitment to uphold the ITAR/EAR by executive and upper management is important. This can be exhibited by incorporating a commitment to comply with all EAR/ITAR compliance in the corporate policy.

DO file with AES for all controlled exports, develop a formal AES training manual and require new employees to take a certification quiz prior to initial filing.

DO keep records pertaining to the export transaction such as purchase order, invoices, and other sales documents, end-use certificates, shippers export declarations and end-user screening results. ITAR requires that applicants keep a record of all information furnished for a license approval for not less than 5 years from the date of report. EAR also requires a 5 year minimum record retention period.

DO have a global system for compliance. As companies go global, computer networks that tie these various international locations together (and increase the flow of communication and information) can also be a gateway for providing unintended access to controlled data and technology. Maintain an effective compliance program that ensures that computer networks do not transfer or disclose controlled information or technology to unauthorized users.

DO have a procedure for screening countries, international carriers, and countries.

DO have a documented training program for company employees for export control laws and regulations.

DO monitor various departments such as shipping, receiving and customer service to ensure compliance.

DO keep the phrases "due diligence" and "criminal and civil penalties" in your vocabulary arsenal.

> *T*IP! When applying for a license try not to bring out the hidden lawyer within, and use convoluted terminology. State your points clearly and concisely. Focus on the scope of the transaction, countries involved, end use and end-user.

Shipper's Export Declaration (SED) Compliance

DO NOT forget this small yet important step before exporting - file an SED via the Automated Export System (AES). In order to use AES, apply directly to the Census Bureau.

SEDs are used for two main reasons. The first is to allow the Census Bureau to collect trade statistics. The second is to allow the Bureau of Industry and Security for export control tracking. An SED must be filed for almost all exports with certain exceptions noted Part 758 of the EAR.

However, most pertinent to you is that an SED must be submitted for ALL exports going out on license regardless of the value or destination. For commercial shipments with exemptions from a license to export, simply note "NLR" (no license required) on the shipping documents (such as the billing of lading or airway bill).   In the event you do need a license, input the license number and expiration date in AES.

DO include a Destination and Control Statement (DCS) on your company's invoices, bills of lading, air waybills or other type of visible export documents. If you followed the correct steps and checked the end-user prior to shipping, the following statement makes the buyer aware that anything done to the article after release from your custody is still bound by the laws and regulations of the EAR.

> *"These commodities, technology or software were exported from the United States in accordance with Export Administration Regulations. Diversion contrary to U.S. law is prohibited."*

Many shippers are under the belief this is optional statement; however, according to part 758.6 of the EAR, it is obligatory.

Preparing for an Audit

Hopefully, after reading the contents of this book, you have a strong foundation of knowledge in ITAR and EAR, and of the resources you'll need for further research. The DDTC and BIS websites contain a vast amount of information and resources to further assist you.   However, in the event that your company is audited, you should have the following in place. Auditors will be looking out for the following. Consider this your Compliance Safelist:

- Maintain license applications and all accompanying supporting documentation for required period.

- Establish company U.S. Export Control Procedure.

- Establish an International Travel Procedure that controls the transfer of data amongst employees traveling internationally.

- If you have foreign national employees and/or visitors, establish a Technology Control Plan and Visitor Process that enforces this plan such as badge identification and visitor sign in and screening process.

- Document screening process for international customers.

- Apart from U.S. Export Control Procedures, have an ITAR policy that expresses the company's commitment to compliance with U.S. export regulation by senior official/CEO of the company.

- Even if a second party is doing so on your companies behalf, verify and retain all SED via AES license shipments are filed by the company.

- Track and monitor articles shipped out 'in furtherance of an agreement' to make sure they do not exceed value amounts specified on agreement i.e. TAA/ MLA.

- Provide initial notification of export according to ITAR 123.22 (b)(3)(ii) for Technical Assistance Agreements.

- Maintain consistent and documented training of your firm's Empowered Official and applicable departments.

- **HR:** Incorporate export control screening into the hiring process, and screen all potential hires against the Restricted Parties Lists.

- **IT:** Identify where controlled technical data is contained within the information system and restrict access to foreign nationals without authorization.

- **Contracts/Purchasing:** Inform customers, intermediate consignees and end users about reexport and retransfer restrictions, be aware of restrictions upon countries and parties with whom you deal, and screen all potential suppliers against Restricted Parties Lists.

- **Marketing and Sales:** International travelers with laptops should not contain controlled data without authorization. If attending a meeting in which controlled data may or will be discussed, ensure that all foreign nationals in attendance are authorized.

- **Shipping:** For controlled goods, confirm that the shipment is authorized by a valid license or exemption Properly document the export on all required export documentation Ensure destination control statement is included on the shipment documentation. Close out TAA that are not being used and retain records according to stipulations.

- Conduct periodically internal audits of the compliance and other departments to gauge the effectiveness of the compliance program.

- If your company incorporates (at a mimimum) the initiatives defined in this Chapter, then you are well on the way to a strong compliance program, managing corporate risk and if the occasion arises a successful audit.

USEFUL DEFINITIONS

Automated Export System (AES): An electronic filing of Shipper's Export Declarations (SEDs) for census purposes.

Bureau of Industry and Security (BIS): A regulatory agency responsible for the licensing and monitoring of items for export for commercial and dual use i.e., commercial and military applications.

Commerce Control List (CCL): A list of items controlled under the Bureau of Industry and Security that can be found in part 774 of the EAR.

Denied Persons List: A list of individuals reported to have violated U.S. export clause and as a result, transactions with there persons are prohibited.

Commerce Country Chart: Established the licensing requirements based on end destination and reason for control. Located in the EAR part 738.

Commodity Jurisdiction: A process that determines the jurisdiction of the USML.

Consignee: The individual the commodity is delivered to by carrier.

Entity List: Normally contains entities and countries known to proliferate weapons of mass destruction and are prohibited from conducting any transactions.

Defense Article: An article classified under the USML.

Dual Use Good: An article that has both commercial and military applications.

Empowered Official: An individual within an organization assigned to sign and process license applications on behalf of the company. This individual must understand the provisions of the ITAR and have the authority to stop, inquire, and verify the legality of an export transaction. An empowered official can be held liable for ITAR violations.

Export: The physical action of shipping an article to a foreign destination but also includes transferring controlled commodities to foreign persons via oral communication, writing, fax, email, visually or physical exchange. It is also the movement of goods through regular mail, hand carried items on an airplane, set of schematics sent via email international and/or controlled software uploaded or downloaded.

End-user: The individual that receives and ultimately uses the exported item.

Export Control Classification Number (ECCN): An alphanumeric number that assist in indentifying items controlled by the Commerce Control List of the BIS.

Export License: Approval documentation issued by the appropriate agency that allows the applicant to export a regulated article, data or service.

Foreign intermediate consignee: Individual or entity that will receive article during the course of shipment to the temp/perm end-user.

International Traffic and Arms Regulations (ITAR): Controls the exports of articles, services and related technical data that are military or more specifically, possess military specification.

Manufacturing Licensing Agreement: Grants a U.S. person to allow a foreign person/company to manufacture defense article or perform a service abroad.

Munitions List (USML): Articles, services or data determined to be defense articles and defense services pursuant to the Arms Export Control Act.

Office of Foreign Assets Control (OFAC): Part of the U.S. Department of Treasury licensed exports to certain embargoed countries and sanctioned individuals and organizations.

Schedule B: 10-digit number commodity codes used to identify exported products for trade statistics purposes.

Shipper's Export Declaration (SED): Prior to mandatory AES, the SED was a document submitted, under certain circumstances, when exporting an article for U.S. trade statistics purposes and enforcing Export regulations.

Technical Data: Can be in the form of diagrams, engineering designs, blue prints, plans, diagrams, models etc.

ACRONYMS

AES: Automated Export System

BIS: Bureau of Industry and Security

CCL: Commerce Control List

DDTC: Directorate of Defense Trade Controls

EAR: Export Administration Regulations

ECCN: Export Control Classification Number

ITAR: International Traffic and Arms Regulations

MLA: Manufacturing Licensing Agreement

OFAC: Office of Foreign Assets Control

SED: Shipper's Export Declaration

TAA: Technical Assistance Agreement

TCP: Technology Control Plan

USML: United States Munitions List

Appendix A
EXPORT LICENSING PROCESS CHART

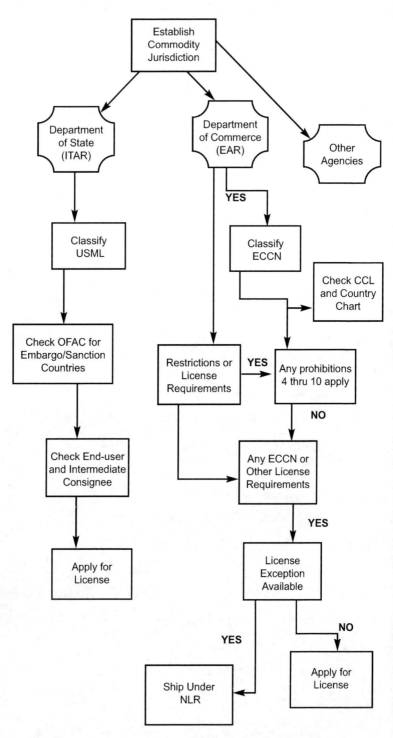

Appendix B

DSP-5 FORM

http://www.pmddtc.state.gov/DTRADE/index.html

Receive this code after registration. You will need it for every application.

This should match up with end-use documents on file.

If the port changes after license is issued and approved, refer to 123.22 ITAR.

DSP-5, Page 1 of 4

SEAL	Signature	DATE ISSUED	
License is hereby granted to the applicant for the described commodity to be permanently exported from the United States. This license may be revoked, suspended or amended by the Secretary of State without prior notice whenever the Secretary deems such action advisable.		LICENSE NO.	LICENSE VALID FOR MONTHS FROM ABOVE DATE

UNITED STATES OF AMERICA DEPARTMENT OF STATE

APPLICATION/LICENSE FOR PERMANENT EXPORT OF UNCLASSIFIED
DEFENSE ARTICLES AND RELATED UNCLASSIFIED TECHNICAL DATA

*1. Date Prepared	* 2. PM/DDTC Applicant/ Registrant Code	* 3. Country of Ultimate Destination:		* 4. Probable Port of Exit from U.S.:
		NOTE: You may only select 1 country as the ultimate destination if the commodity(ies) being shipped include Hardware type.		

5. Applicant's Name, Address, ZIP Code, Telephone Number

*Applicant is: ☐ Government ☐ Manufacturer ☐ Exporter ☐ Subsidiary

*Name

*Attention

*Address

*City

*State _____ * ZIP Code _____

*Telephone # _____ Ext.

6. Name, agency and telephone number of U.S. Government personnel (not PM/DDTC) familiar with the commodity.

Name

Telephone # _____ Ext.

Agency

[Add]

* 7. Name and telephone numbers of applicant contact if U.S. Government needs additional information.

*Name

*Telephone # _____ Ext.

[Add]

8. Description of Transaction:

*a. This application represents: ☐ ONLY completely new shipment ☐ ONLY the unshipped balance under license numbers

b. This application has related license numbers: ☐

c. This application is in reference to an agreement: ☐

*d. Commodity is being financed under: ☐ Foreign Military Sale ☐ Foreign Military Financing ☐ Grant Aid Program ☐ Not Applicable

*e. This application is related to a disclosure filed with Defense Trade Controls Compliance ☐ No ☐ Yes

Enter Compliance Disclosure Number: _____

Line Item #	*9. Quantity	*10. Commodity	* 11. USML Category Number
1	Unit Type		Category ____ ____ ____
			Item is SME and DSP-83 is required ☐
			Is a DSP-83 attached? _____
			If SME, and DSP-83 is not attached, state why.
			*12. $ Value — Unit Price _____ Line Item Total _____
		Defense Article Type _____	
	[Add] ☐	*13. TOTAL VALUE (Sum of All Pages) $	

Check this box if the article on the USML has an * next to it. This means it's considered significant military equipment . If so, attach DSP-83 as supporting documentation.

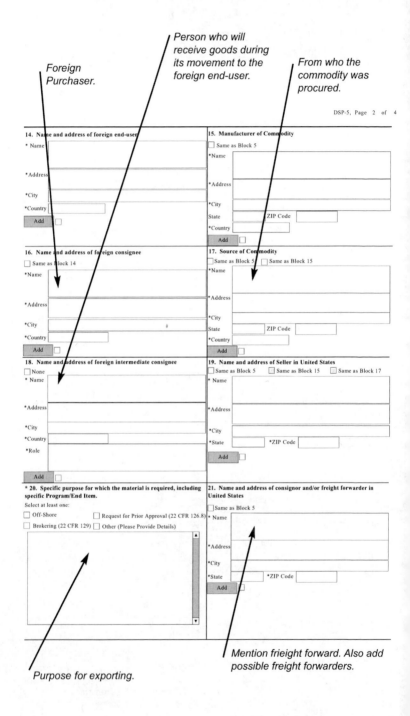

Foreign Purchaser.

Person who will receive goods during its movement to the foreign end-user.

From who the commodity was procured.

DSP-5, Page 2 of 4

14. Name and address of foreign end-user
* Name
*Address
*City
*Country
Add

15. Manufacturer of Commodity
☐ Same as Block 5
*Name
*Address
*City
State   ZIP Code
*Country
Add

16. Name and address of foreign consignee
☐ Same as Block 14
*Name
*Address
*City
*Country
Add

17. Source of Commodity
☐ Same as Block 5   ☐ Same as Block 15
*Name
*Address
*City
State   ZIP Code
*Country
Add

18. Name and address of foreign intermediate consignee
☐ None
* Name
*Address
*City
*Country
*Role
Add

19. Name and address of Seller in United States
☐ Same as Block 5   ☐ Same as Block 15   ☑ Same as Block 17
* Name
*Address
*City
*State   *ZIP Code
Add

* 20. Specific purpose for which the material is required, including specific Program/End Item.
Select at least one:
☐ Off-Shore   ☐ Request for Prior Approval (22 CFR 126.8)
☐ Brokering (22 CFR 129) ☐ Other (Please Provide Details)

21. Name and address of consignor and/or freight forwarder in United States
☐ Same as Block 5
* Name
*Address
*City
*State   *ZIP Code
Add

Mention frieght forward. Also add possible freight forwarders.

Purpose for exporting.

APPENDIX B

Digitally sign at this point. You are testifying to the validity of the the information and that meet the criteria of 120.25 of ITAR.

DSP-5

22. Applicant's statement

I

an empowered official (ITAR 120.25) or an official of a foreign government entity in the U.S., hereby apply for a license to complete the transaction described above; warrant the truth of all statements made herein; and acknowledge, understand and will comply with the provisions of Title 22 CFR, 120-130, and any conditions and limitations imposed.

I am authorized by the applicant to certify the following in compliance with 22 CFR 126.13:

(1) Neither applicant, its chief executive officer, president, vice presidents, other senior officers or officials (e.g., comptroller, treasurer, general counsel) nor any member of its board of directors is:

    (a) the subject of an indictment for or has been convicted of violating any of the U.S. criminal statutes enumerated in 22 CFR120.27 since the effective date of the Arms Export Control Act, Public Law 94-329, 90 Stat. 729 (June 30, 1976); or

    (b) ineligible to contract with, or to receive a license or other approval to import defense articles or defense services from, or to receive an export license or other approval from any agency of the U.S. Government;

(2) To the best of the applicant's knowledge, no party to the export as defined in 22 CFR 126.7 (e) has been convicted of violating any of the U.S. criminal statutes enumerated in 22 CFR 120.27 since the effective date of the Arms Export Control Act, Public Law 94-329, 90 Stat. 729 (June 30, 1976); or is ineligible to contract with, or to receive a license or other approval to import defense articles or defense services from, or to receive an export lisence or other approval from any agency of the U.S. Government.

*22 CFR 126.13 Certification (Select one)

    a. I am authorized by the applicant to certify that the applicant and all the parties to the transaction can meet in full the conditions of 22 CFR § 126.13 as listed above.

    b. I am authorized by the applicant to certify to 22 CFR § 126.13. The applicant or one of the parties of the transaction cannot meet one or more of the conditions of 22 CFR § 126.13 as listed above. A request for an exception to policy, as described in Section 127.11 of the ITAR, is attached.

    c. I am authorized by the applicant to certify to 22 CFR § 126.13. The applicant or one of the parties of the transaction cannot meet one or more of the conditions of 22 CFR § 126.13 as listed above. However that party has met the conditions imposed by the Directorate of Defense Trade Controls in order to resume standard submission of applications, not requiring an exception to policy as described in Section 127.11 of the ITAR.

    d. I am not authorized by the applicant to certify the conditions of 22 CFR § 126.13. The applicant and all of the parties to the transaction can meet in full the conditions of 22 CFR § 126.13 as listed above. Please see the attached letter from an official that is authorized by the applicant to certify to the conditions of 22 CFR § 126.13.

    e. I am not authorized by the applicant to certify the conditions of 22 CFR § 126.13. The applicant or one of the parties of the transaction cannot meet one or more of the conditions of 22 CFR § 126.13 as listed above. A request for an exception to policy, as described in Section 127.11 of the ITAR, and a letter from an official that is authorized by the applicant to certify to the conditions of 22 CFR § 126.13 are attached.

    f. I am not authorized by the applicant to certify the conditions of 22 CFR § 126.13. The applicant or one of the parties of the transaction cannot meet one or more of the conditions of 22 CFR § 126.13 as listed above. However that party has met the conditions imposed by the Directorate of Defense Trade Controls in order to resume standard submission of applications, not requiring an exception to policy as described in Section 127.11 of the ITAR. Please see the attached letter from an official that is authorized by the applicant to certify to the conditions of 22 CFR § 126.13.

*Compliance with 22 CFR 130 (Select one)

    This transaction does not meet the requirements of 22 CFR 130.2.

    This transaction meets the requirements of 22 CFR 130.2. The applicant or its vendors **have not** paid, nor offered, nor agreed to pay, in respect of any sale for which a license or approval is requested, political contributions, fees or commissions in amounts as specified in 22 CFR 130.9(a).

    The applicant or its vendors **have** paid, or offered, or agreed to pay, in respect of any safle for which a license or approval is requested, political contributions, fees or commissions in amounts as specified in 22 CFR 130.9(a). Information required under 22 CFR 130.10 is attached.

    I am not authorized by the applicant to certify the conditions of 22 CFR 130.9(a). Please see the attached letter for such certification.

*Signature

    Signature

23. License to be to: (Enter name, address and phone number)

[This block is inactive on electronic form.]

    Same as Block 5   Hold for Pickup

Name

Address

City

State   ZIP Code

Telephone #

Appendix C

DSP-5 FORM/FOREIGN NATIONAL
http://www.pmddtc.state.gov/DTRADE/index.html

Select type of control / USML.

DSP-5, Page 1 of 4

SEAL	DATE ISSUED	
Signature		LICENSE VALID FOR
License is hereby granted to the applicant for the described commodity to be permanently exported from the United States. This license may be revoked, suspended or amended by the Secretary of State without prior notice whenever the Secretary deems such action advisable.	LICENSE NO.	MONTHS FROM ABOVE DATE

UNITED STATES OF AMERICA   DEPARTMENT OF STATE

APPLICATION/LICENSE FOR PERMANENT EXPORT OF UNCLASSIFIED
DEFENSE ARTICLES AND RELATED UNCLASSIFIED TECHNICAL DATA

*1. Date Prepared 04/17/2009	* 2. PM/DDTC Applicant/ Registrant Code	* 3. Country of Ultimate Destination:	* 4. Probable Port of Exit from U.S.:

NOTE: You may only select 1 country as the ultimate destination if the commodity(ies) being shipped include Hardware type.

5. Applicant's Name, Address, ZIP Code, Telephone Number

*Applicant is: Government   Manufacturer   Exporter   Subsidiary

*Name

*Attention

*Address

*City

*State   * ZIP Code

*Telephone #   Ext.

6. Name, agency and telephone number of U.S. Government personnel (not PM/DDTC) familiar with the commodity.

Name

Telephone #   Ext.

Agency

7. Name and telephone numbers of applicant contact if U.S. Government needs additional information.

*Name

*Telephone #   Ext.

8. Description of Transaction:

*a. This application represents: ONLY completely new shipment   ONLY the unshipped balance under license number

b. This application has related license numbers:

c. This application is in reference to an agreement:

*d. Commodity is being financed under: _ Foreign Military Sale _ Foreign Military Financing _ Grant Aid Program _ Not Applicable

*e. This application is related to a disclosure filed with Defense Trade Controls Compliance No Yes

Enter Compliance Disclosure Number:

Line Item #	*9. Quantity	*10. Commodity	* 11. USML Category Number
1	Unit Type		Category Sub Commodity Code
			Item is SME and DSP-83 is required
			Is a DSP-83 attached?
			If SME, and DSP-83 is not attached, state why.
		Defense Article Type	*12. $ Value Unit Price Line Item Total
		*13. TOTAL VALUE (Sum of All Pages) $	

Select type of article or data.

Specify USML data FN will have access/exposure to.

Value of data.

APPENDIX C

FN return address in home country.

IF FN is a national of another country, provide address.

If FN already is in the U.S., address here.

DSP-5, Page 2 of 4

14. Name and address of foreign end-user
* Name
*Address
*City
*Country

15. Manufacturer of Commodity
Same as Block 5
*Name
*Address
*City
State   ZIP Code
*Country

16. Name and address of foreign consignee
Same as Block 14
*Name
*Address
*City
*Country

17. Source of Commodity
Same as Block 5   Same as Block 15
*Name
*Address
*City
State   ZIP Code
*Country

18. Name and address of foreign intermediate consignee
None
* Name
*Address
*City
*Country
*Role

19. Name and address of Seller in United States
Same as Block 5   Same as Block 15   Same as Block 17
* Name
*Address
*City
*State   *ZIP Code

* 20. Specific purpose for which the material is required, including specific Program/End Item.
Select at least one:
Off-Shore   Request for Prior Approval (22 CFR 126.8)
Brokering (22 CFR 129)   Other (Please Provide Details)

21. Name and address of consignor and/or freight forwarder in United States
Same as Block 5
* Name
*Address
*City
*State   *ZIP Code

Include specifics of program and end-use.

113

Appendix D

DSP-61 TEMPORARY IMPORT FORM
http://www.pmddtc.state.gov/DTRADE/index.html

Expected U.S. Customs port where article will arrive.

Expected U.S. Port where article will depart.

DSP-61, Page 1 of 4

SEAL	
_____ Signature	DATE ISSUED
License is hereby granted to the applicant for the described commodity to be shipped to the United States in transit to indicated destination. This license may be revoked, suspended or amended by the Secretary of State without prior notice whenever the Secretary deems such action advisable.	LICENSE NO _____ LICENSE VALID FOR _____ MONTHS FROM ABOVE DATE

UNITED STATES OF AMERICA   DEPARTMENT OF STATE
APPLICATION/LICENSE FOR TEMPORARY IMPORT OF UNCLASSIFIED DEFENSE ARTICLES

*1. Date prepared 04/23/2009	* 2. PM/DDTC Applicant/Registrant Code	* 3. Foreign country from which shipped:	* 4. U.S. port of import
		* 5. Foreign Country of Ultimate Destination:	* 6. U.S. port of export

7. Name, agency and telephone number of U.S. Government personnel (not PM/DDTC) familiar with the commodity

Name _____
Agency _____
Telephone # _____ Ext. _____

8. Applicant's Name, Address, ZIP Code, and Telephone Number

*Applicant is: ☐ Manufacturer ☐ Exporter ☐ Government ☐ Subsidiary

*Name _____

9. Name and telephone numbers of applicant contact if U.S. Government needs additional information

*Name _____
*Telephone # _____ Ext. _____
[Add]

*Attention _____
*Address _____
*City _____
*State _____ *ZIP Code _____
*Telephone # _____ Ext. _____

10. Description of Transaction

A. ☐ The identical commodity was licensed to the country in Block 3 under license number(s).

B. ☐ The identical commodity was licensed to other countries under license number(s).

C. ☐ The identical commodity was denied to the country in Block 5 under voided license number(s).

D. ☐ The identical commodity was never licensed for this applicant.

E. ☐ This transaction is in furtherance of agreement number(s).

F. ☐ The transaction is in support of agreement number(s).

* G. This application is related to a disclosure filed with Defense Trade Controls Compliance ☐ No ☐ Yes

   Enter Compliance Disclosure Number: _____

Line Item #	*11. Quantity	*12a. Commodity	*12b. The commodity is a _____
1	Unit Type		*12c. Identify the commodity for which it is intended ☐ None
	*13. USML Cat. Number Category Sub Commodity Code		*14. $ Value Unit Price Line Item Total
	[Add]		*15. TOTAL VALUE (Sum of All Pages) $ 0

For exports in transist be sure to include a document that verifies the purchase, foreign end-use, user, price and quanity.

APPENDIX D

Name and address of responsible party shipping commodity in foreign country.

DSP-61, Page 2 of 4

16. Name and address of owner/end-user of commodity in foreign country from which shipped	17. Manufacturer of Commodity ☐ Same as Block 8 ☐ Unknown
*Name	*Name
*Address	*Address
*City	*City
*Country	State ▪ ZIP Code
	*Country

18. Name and address of consignor in foreign country from which shipped	19. Source of Commodity ☐ Same as Block 8 ☐ Same as Block 17
*Name	*Name
*Address	*Address
*City	*City
*Country	State ▪ ZIP Code
	*Country

20. Name and address of foreign intermediate consignee ☐ None	21. Name and address of U.S. intermediate consignee ☐ Same as Block 8
*Name	*Name
*Address	*Address
*City	*City
*Country	*State ▪ *ZIP Code

22. Name and address of consignee in foreign country of ultimate destination ☐ None	*23. Specific purpose for which the article or hardware is temporarily imported
*Name	a. Select all that apply: ☐ Overhaul/Repair ☐ Modification/Upgrade ☐ Other (Provide Details)
*Address	
*City	
*Country	

24. Name and address of end user in foreign country of ultimate destination ☐ Same as Block 16	
*Name	b. ☐ Return to country in Block 16 ☐ Transshipment to third country
*Address	
*City	
*Country	

Reason why it is being temporily imported.

115

Appendix E

DSP-73 TEMPORARY EXPORT FORM
http://www.pmddtc.state.gov/DTRADE/index.html

Temporary export of hardware can have more than one ultimate destination but if the exports are going to seperate regions (for example to Africa and Asia), then seperate applications for each region should be submitted.

Items where article will be temporarily exported must match block 22 end-user.

DSP-73, Page 1 of 4

SEAL		DATE ISSUED	
Signature			

License is hereby granted to the applicant for the described commodity to depart from the United States for temporary export and return to the United States. This license may be revoked, suspended or amended by the Secretary of State without prior notice whenever the Secretary deems such action advisable.

LICENSE NO. | **LICENSE VALID FOR MONTHS FROM ABOVE DATE**

UNITED STATES OF AMERICA DEPARTMENT OF STATE
APPLICATION/LICENSE FOR TEMPORARY EXPORT OF UNCLASSIFIED DEFENSE ARTICLES

*1. Date Prepared	*2. PM/DDTC Applicant/Registrant Code	*3. Select One: Single departure and return / Series of departures and return	*4. Specific countries of sojourn

5. Applicant's Name, Address, ZIP Code and Telephone Number
*Applicant is: ☐ Government ☐ Manufacturer ☐ Exporter
☐ Subsidiary

*Name
*Attention
*Address
*City
*State   *ZIP Code
*Telephone #   Ext

*6. Probable port of exit from U.S.
*7. Probable port of entry into U.S.
*8. Probable date of first exit from U.S.   mm/dd/yyyy
*9. Probable date of final entry into U.S.   mm/dd/yyyy

10a. Name and telephone numbers of individual(s) to contact if U.S. Government needs additional information.
*Name
*Telephone #   Ext
Add

10b. Name, agency and telephone numbers of U.S. Government personnel (not PM/DDTC) familiar with the commodity.
Name
Telephone #   Ext
Agency
Add

11. Description of Transaction

A. This application represents: ☐ ONLY completely new shipment ☐ ONLY renewal of previously issued license no.

B. This application has related license no(s):

Line Item #	*12. Quantity	*13. Commodity	*14. USML Category Number
1	Unit Type		Category Sub Commodity Code
			*15. $ Value Unit Price Line Item Total

Add

*16. Total Value (Sum of All Pages) $

Expected date of final entry, all exits and entries must not exceed license validity period.

Match with Block 4

Provide individual or entity that will receive article in the process of shipping to temporary end-user.

DSP-73, Page 2 of 4

17. Manufacturer of Commodity		18. Name and address of foreign intermediate consignee	
_ Same as Block 5	Unknown	None	
*Name		*Name	
*Address		*Address	
*City		*City	
State	ZIP Code	*Country	
*Country		*Role	

19. Source of Commodity		20. Name and address of temporary foreign consignee	
_ Same as Block 5	Same as Block 17	None	
*Name		*Name	
*Address		*Address	
*City		*City	
State	ZIP Code	*Country	
*Country			

21. Name and address of consignor and/or freight forwarder in United States		22. Name and address of temporary foreign end-user	
Same as Block 5		Same as Block 20	
*Name		*Name	
*Address		*Address	
*City		*City	
*State	*ZIP Code	*Country	

*23. Specific purpose of temporary export	*24. Is the article being exported an Aircraft or Vessel?
Request for Prior Approval (22 CFR § 126.8)	Yes No
	Note: Blocks 25 - 29 are on another page and are only displayed if there is a "Yes" response to Block 24.

If the article is considered SME, applicant should select Request For Prior Approval

Appendix F

SAMPLE TECHNOLOGY CONTROL PLAN

Scope: The procedures contained in this plan apply to all elements of the _____ (insert company name and address). Disclosure of unclassified and/or classified information to foreign persons in a visitor status or in the course of their employment by _____ (insert company name) is considered an export disclosure under the International Traffic in Arms Regulations (ITAR) and requires a licensing by the Department of State.

Purpose: To delineate and inform employees and visitors of _____ (insert company name) the controls necessary to ensure that no transfer of technical information or data or a defense service (as defined in ITAR paragraphs §120.10 & §120.9) occurs unless authorized by the Directorate of Defense Trade Controls (DDTC).

Background: _____ (insert company name) _____ (explain the products and services the company provide (e.g., designs, manufactures, integrates...). Reference customers it provides products and/or services to (including foreign customers).

Foreign Persons: No foreign person will be given access to unclassified and/or classified material on any project or program that involves the disclosure of technical data as defined in ITAR paragraph 120.10 until that individual's license authority has been approved by the Office of Defense Trade Controls Licensing (DTCL).

_____ (insert company name) employees who have supervisory responsibilities for foreign persons must receive an export control/licensing briefing that addresses relevant ITAR requirements as they pertain to classified and controlled unclassified information.

Foreign Persons: - Foreign persons employed by, assigned to (extended visit) or visiting _____ (insert name of company), shall receive a briefing that addressees the following items:

> - Prior to the release of classified material or controlled unclassified information to a foreign person an export authorization issued by DTCL needs to be obtained by _____ (insert company name).

> - Ensure foreign persons adhere to the _____'s (insert company name) security rules, policies and procedures and in-plant personnel regulations.

> - Outline the specific information that has been authorized for release to them.

> - Address the _____'s (insert name of the company) in-plant regulations for the use of facsimile, automated information systems and reproduction machines.

> - Any classified information they are authorized to have access and need to forward overseas will be submitted to the _____'s (insert company name) security department for transmission through government-to-government channels.

- Information received at _____ (insert company name) for the foreign national and information that the foreign national needs to forward from _____ (insert company name) shall be prepared in English.

- Violations of security procedures and in-plant regulations committed by foreign nationals are subject to _____ (insert company name) sanctions.

Access Controls for Foreign Nationals: Address how foreign nationals will be controlled within the company's premises, for example:

a. Badges: (if necessary, address procedures, e.g., composition of the badge, identification on badge that conveys that the individual is a foreign national, privileges and so forth).

b. Escorts: (if necessary, address escort procedures.) NOTE: _____ (insert name of company) supervisors of foreign persons shall ensure that foreign nationals are escorted in accordance with U.S. Government and _____ (insert name of company) regulations.

c. Establishment of a segregated work area(s), if necessary.

Export Controlled Information: List specific elements of export controlled information, both classified and unclassified, that can be disclosed to foreign nationals and the program(s) the foreign national is supporting

Non-Disclosure Statement: All foreign persons shall sign a non-disclosure statement that acknowledges that classified and controlled unclassified information will not be further disclosed, exported or transmitted by the individual to any foreign national or foreign country unless DDTC authorizes such a disclosure and the receiving party is appropriately cleared in accordance with its government's personnel security system.

Supervisory Responsibilities: Supervisors of cleared personnel and foreign national employees and foreign national visitors shall ensure that the employees and visitors are informed of and cognizant of the following:

- Technical data or defense services that require an export authorization is not transmitted, shipped, mailed, hand-carried (or any other means of transmission) unless an export authorization has already been obtained by _____ (insert company name) and the transmission procedures follows U.S. Government regulations.

- Individuals are cognizant of all regulations concerning the handling and safeguarding of classified information and controlled unclassified information. (NOTE: Companies may also want to address company propriety and other types of unclassified information that require mandated controls.

- Individuals execute a technology control plan (TCP) briefing form acknowledging that they have received a copy of the TCP and were briefed on the contents of the plan (Attachment B).

- U.S. citizen employees are knowledgeable of the information that can be disclosed or accessed by foreign nationals.

_____
_____
_____
_____

_____
_____
_____
_____

Employee Responsibilities: All _____ (insert name of company) employees who interface with foreign nationals shall receive a copy of the TCP and a briefing that addresses the following:

- Documents under their jurisdiction that contain technical data are not released to or accessed by any employee, visitor, or subcontractor who is a foreign national unless an export authorization has been obtained by _____(insert company name) in accordance with the ITAR or the Export Administration Regulations (EAR).

- If there is any question as to whether or not an export authorization is required, contact the Facility Security Officer promptly.

- Technical information or defense services cannot be forwarded or provided to a foreign national regardless of the foreign nationals location unless an export authorization has been approved by DDTC and issued to _____(insert company's name).

Appendix G
ELIGIBILITY LETTER

Appendix G

Company Letterhead

Date:

U.S. Dept of State Director
Office of Defense Trade Controls Licensing
2401 E. Street NW, SA-1, Room H1200
Washington, DC 20522-0112

Re: Eligibility Letter

Dear Director:

I, (name of empowered official), am a U.S. person as defined in ITAR 120.15 and I am a responsible official empowered by the applicant to certify the following in compliance with ITAR 126.31.

Neither the intending registrant, chief executive officer, president, vice-presidents, other senior officers or officers (e.g. comptroller, treasurer, general counsel) nor any member of board of director is:

> 1. Indicted for or convicted of violating any of the U.S. criminal statues enumerated in ITAR 120.27.

> 2. Is ineligible to contract with or receive a license or other approval to import defense articles or defense services from, or to receive an export license or other approval from any agency of the U.S. Government.

> 3. To the best of the applicant's knowledge, no party to the export as defined in 126.7(e) of the ITAR has been convicted of violating any of the U.S. criminal statues enumerated in 120.27 of this subchapter since the effective date of the Arms Export Control Act.

> 4. The natural person signing the application, for the license or other request for approval is a responsible official who has been empowered by the applicant and is a citizen of the United States.

Sincerely,

_____

(Type your name)
Empowered Official, of the Company
Street Address   •   City, State   •   Zip Code
Phone Number   •   E-mail Address

Appendix H

DELIVERY VERIFICATION CERTIFICATE
http://www.bis.doc.gov/licensing/bis647-p.pdf

Form Approved: OMB No. 0694-0016, 0694-0093

FORM BIS-647-P
(REV.4/03)

U.S. DEPARTMENT OF COMMERCE
Bureau of Industry and Security

DELIVERY VERIFICATION CERTIFICATE

Public reporting burden for this collection of information is estimated to average 15 minutes per response,, including the time for reviewing instructions, searching existing data sources, gathering and maintaining the data needed, and completing and reviewing the collection of information. Send comments regarding this burden estimate or any other aspect of this collection of information, including suggestions for reducing the burden, to the Director of Administration, room-3889, Bureau of Industry and Security, U.S. Department of Commerce, Washington, D.C. 20230; and to the Office of Management and Budget Paperwork Reduction Project (0694-0016, 0694-0093) Washington, DC 20503.

Notwithstanding any other provision of law, no person is required to respond to nor shall a person be subject to a penalty for failure to comply with a collection of information subject to the requirements of the Paperwork Reduction Act unless that collection of information displays a currently valid OMB Control Number.

Instructions- When required to obtain a delivery verification, the U.S. Importer shall submit this form in duplicate, to the Customs Office. U.S. importer is required to complete all items on this form except the portion to be completed by the U.S. Customs Service. The Customs Office will certify a Delivery Verification Certificate only after the import has been delivered to the U.S. importer. The duly certified form shall then be dispatched by the U.S. importer to the foreign exporter or otherwise disposed of in accordance with instructions of the exporting country.

No delivery verification may be obtained unless a completed application form has been received. (50 U.S.C App § 2401 et seq.,15 C.F.R. §748)

EXPORTER *(Name and Address)*	This certification applied to the goods described below, shown on
Name	U.S. Department of Commerce International Import Certificate No.
Address	
City State/Country Zip/ Postal Code	**ARRIVED** *(Name of Port)* / **DATE OF ARRIVAL** *(mm/dd/yyyy)*
IMPORTER *(Name and Address)*	**NAME OF SHIP, AIRCRAFT, OR CARRIER** *(Include numbers on bills of lading, airways bills, etc.)*
Name	
Address	
City State/Country Zip/ Postal Code	

DESCRIPTION OF GOODS	QUANTITY	VALUE *(FOB, CIR, etc)*

TO BE COMPLETED BY U.S. CUSTOMS SERVICE		REGION NO.
(Custom's Seal)	CERTIFICATION-It is hereby certified that the importer has produced evidence that the goods specified above have been delivered and brought under the Export Administration Regulations of the United States.	
	Signature	Date

ENTRY	☐ WAREHOUSE ☐ CONSUMPTION	NUMBER	DATE

Appendix I

IMPORT CERTIFICATE
http://www.bis.doc.gov/licensing/facts4.htm

FORM BIS-645P/ATF-4522/DPS-53 (REV 8/02)   Form Approved: OMB No. 0694-0017 - Modele approuvé: OMB No. 0694-0017

U.S. DEPARTMENT OF COMMERCE **Bureau of Industry and Security** **U.S. DEPARTMENT OF THE TREASURY** **Bureau of Alcohol, Tobacco and Firearms** **U.S. DEPARTMENT OF STATE** **Office of Munitions Control**	**INTERNATIONAL IMPORT CERTIFICATE** **(CERTIFICAT INTERNATIONAL D'IMPORTATION)**
NOTE: **Read instructions on the reverse side before completing and submitting this form.** (Lire les instructions au verso avant de remplir et de presenter la présente formule.)	Certificate Number
1. U.S. **Importer/Importateur** (Name and address—Nom et adresse)	FOR U.S. GOVERNMENT USE (Réservé pour le Gouvernement des Etats-Unis)
2. **Exporter/Exportateur** (Name and address—Nom et adresse)	If this form has been approved by the Department of Commerce or the Department of State, it is not valid unless the official seal of the Department of Commerce, or the Department of State, appears in this space. If this form is approved by the Treasury Department, a seal is not required. (Si ce formulaire a été approuvé par le Ministère du Commerce, ou le Ministère des Affaires Etrangères, il n'est pas valide à moins qu'un sceau officiel du Ministère du Commerce ou du Ministère des Affaires Etrangères soit apposé sur le document. Si ce formulaire est approuvé par le Ministère des Finances, un sceau officiel n'est pas nécessaire.

3. Description of goods (Désignation de la Marchandise)	TSUS Anno. No. (Numéro de la liste)	Quantity (Quantité)	Value (Valeur) (FOB, CIF, etc.)

4. Representation and undertaking of U.S. importer or principal

The undersigned hereby represents that he has undertaken to import into the United States of America under a U.S. Consumption Entry or U.S. Warehouse Entry the commodities in quantities described above, or, if the commodities are not so imported into the United States of America, that he will not divert, transship, or reexport them to another destination except with explicit approval of the Department of Commerce, the Department of State, or the Department of the Treasury, as appropriate. The undersigned also undertakes to notify the appropriate Department immediately on any change of fact or intention set forth herein. If a delivery verification is required, the undersigned also undertakes to obtain such verification and make disposition of it in accordance with such requirement. **Any false statement willfully made in this declaration is punishable by fine and imprisonment.** (See experts from U.S. Code on reverse side.)

Déclaration et engagement de l'importateur ou du commettant des Etats-Unis

Le soussigné déclare par la présente qu'il a pris l'engagement d'importer aux Etats-Unis d'Amérique, en vertu d'une Déclaration américaine de Mise en Consommation, ou d'une Declaration américaine d'Entrée en entrepôt, la quantité de produits ci-dessus et que, dans le cas ou ces produits ne seraient pas ainsi importés aux Etats-Unis d'Amérique, il ne le détournera, ne les transbordera, ni les réexportera à destination d'un autre lieu, si ce n'est avec l'approbation explicite du Ministère du Commerce, du Ministère des Affaires Etrangères ou du Ministère des Finances, comme il est requis. Le soussigné prend également l'engagement d'aviser le Ministère intéressé des Etats-Unis de tous changements survenus dans les actes ou les intentions énoncés dans la présente déclaration. Si demande est faite d'une confirmation de la livraison le soussigné prend également l'engagement d'obtenir cette confirmation et d'en disposer de la manière prescrite par cette demande. **Toute fausee déclaration faite intentionnellement expose l'auteur aux pénalités prévues par la loi.** (Voir Extrait du Code des Etats-Unis au verso.)

Type or Print (Prière d'écrire a la machine ou en caractères d imprimerie)	Type or Print (Prière d'écrire a la machine ou en caractères d imprimerie)
Name of Firm or Corporation (Nom de la Firme ou de la Societé)	Name and Title of Authorized Official (Nom et titre de l'agent ou employé autorisé)
Signature of Authorized Official (Signature de l'agent ou employé autorisé)	Date of Signature (Date de la signature)

This document ceases to be valid unless presented to the competent foreign authorities within six months from its date of issue. (Le présent document perd sa validité s'il n'est pas remis aux autorités étrangères compétentes dans un délai de six mois à compter de sa délivrance.)

No import certification may be obtained unless this International Import Certificate has been completed and filed with the appropriate U.S. Government agency (Department of Commerce: 50 U.S.C. app. §2411, E.O. 12214 15 C.F.R. §368; Department of the Treasury; 22 U.S.C. §2778, E.O. 11959, 27 C.F.R. §47; Department of State: 22 U.S.C. 2778, 2779, E.O. 11958, 22 C.F.R. §123). Information furnished herewith is subject to the provisions of Section 12(c) of the Export Administration Act of 1979, 50 U.S.C. app. 2411(c), and its unauthorized disclosure is prohibited by law.

FOR U.S. GOVERNMENT USE (Réservé au Gouvernement des Etats-Unis)

Certification: This is to certify that the above declaration was made to the U.S. Department of Commerce, State, or Treasury through the undersigned designated official thereof and a copy of this certification is placed in the official files.

Certification : Il est certifié par la présente que la déclaration ci-dessus a été faite au Ministère du Commerce, des Affaires Etrangères, ou des Finances des Etats-Unis par l'intermédiaire du fonctionnaire autorisé soussigné de ce Ministère et qu'une copie de ce certificat a été conservée dans les archives officielles.

Signature_____Date_____

Designated Commerce, State, or Treasury Official (Fonctionnaire competent du Ministère du Commerce, d'Etat, ou du Trésor)   Date

USCOMM DC 89-24414

ORIGINAL COPY

Appendix J

STATEMENT BY ULTIMATE CONSIGNEE AND PURCHASER

http://www.bis.doc.gov/licensing/bis711.pdf

FORM **BIS-711** FORM APPROVED UNDER OMB CONTROL NO. 0694-0021, 0694-0093	U.S. DEPARTMENT OF COMMERCE BUREAU OF INDUSTRY AND SECURITY Information furnished herewith is subject to the provisions of Section 12(c) of the Export Administration Act of 1979, as amended, 50 U.S.C. app 2411(c) and its unauthorized disclosure is prohibited by law.	DATE RECEIVED (Leave Blank)

STATEMENT BY ULTIMATE CONSIGNEE AND PURCHASER

1. ULTIMATE CONSIGNEE	CITY	
ADDRESS LINE 1	COUNTRY	
ADDRESS LINE 2	POSTAL CODE	TELEPHONE OR FAX

2. DISPOSITION OR USE OF ITEMS BY ULTIMATE CONSIGNEE NAMED IN BLOCK 1

We certify that the items: *(left mouse click in the appropriate box below)*

A. ☐ Will be used by us (as capital equipment) in the form in which received in a manufacturing process in the country named in Block 1 and will not be reexported or incorporated into an end product.

B. ☐ Will be processed or incorporated by us into the following product (s) _____ to be manufactured in the country named in Block 1 for distribution in _____

C. ☐ Will be resold by us in the form in which received in the country named in Block 1 for use or consumption therein. The specific end-use by my customer will be _____

D. ☐ Will be reexported by us in the form in which received to _____

E. ☐ Other (describe fully) _____

NOTE: If BOX (D) is checked, acceptance of this form by the Bureau of Industry and Security as a supporting document for license applications shall not be construed as an authorization to reexport the items to which the form applies unless specific approval has been obtained from the Bureau of Industry and Security for such export.

3. NATURE OF BUSINESS OF ULTIMATE CONSIGNEE NAMED IN BLOCK 1

A. The nature of our usual business is _____

B. Our business relationship with the U.S. exporter is _____

and we have had this business relationship for ____ year(s).

4. ADDITIONAL INFORMATION

5. ASSISTANCE IN PREPARING STATEMENT

STATEMENT OF ULTIMATE CONSIGNEE AND PURCHASER
We certify that all of the facts contained in this statement are true and correct to the best of our knowledge and we do not know of any additional facts which are inconsistent with the above statement. We shall promptly send a supplemental statement to the U.S. Exporter, disclosing any change of facts or intentions set forth in this statement which occurs after the statement has been prepared and forwarded, except as specifically authorized by the U.S. Export Administration Regulations (15 CFR parts 730-774), or by prior written approval of the Bureau of Industry and Security, we will not reexport, resell, or otherwise dispose of any items approved on a license supported by this statement (1) to any country not approved for export as brought to our attention by means of a bill of lading, commercial invoice, or any other means, or(2) to any person if we know that it will result directly or indirectly, in disposition of the items contrary to the representations made in this statement or contrary to Export Administration Regulations.

6. SIGNATURE OF OFFICIAL OF ULTIMATE CONSIGNEE	7. NAME OF PURCHASER
NAME OF OFFICIAL	SIGNATURE OF PURCHASER
TITLE OF OFFICIAL	NAME OF OFFICIAL
DATE *(mmmm,dd,yyyy)*	TITLE OF OFFICIAL
CERTIFICATION FOR USE OF U.S. EXPORTER - We certify that no corrections, additions, or alterations were made on this form by us after the form was signed by the (ultimate consignee)(purchaser).	DATE *(mmmm,dd,yyyy)*
8. NAME OF EXPORTER	SIGNATURE OF PERSON AUTHORIZED TO CERTIFY FOR EXPORTER
NAME OF PERSON SIGNING THIS DOCUMENT	TITLE OF PERSON SIGNING THIS DOCUMENT / DATE *(mmmm,dd,yyyy)*

We acknowledge that the making of any false statements or concealment of any material fact in connection with this statement may result in imprisonment or fine, or both and denial, in whole or in part, of participation in U.S. exports and reexports.

Public reporting burden for this collection of information is estimated to average 15 minutes per response plus one minute for recordkeeping, including the time for reviewing instruments, searching existing data sources, gathering and maintaining the data needed, and completing and reviewing the collection of information. Send comments regarding this burden estimate or any other aspect of this collection of information, including suggestions for reducing this burden, to the Director of Administration, Room 3889, Bureau of Industry and Security, U.S. Department of Commerce, Washington, DC 20230, and to the Office of Management and Budget Paperwork Reduction Project (0694-0021, 0694-0093), Washington, D.C. 20503. Notwithstanding any other provision of law, no person is obligated to respond to nor shall a person be subject to a penalty for failure to comply with a collection of information subject to the Paperwork Reduction Act unless that collection of information displays a currently valid OMB Control Number.

Appendix K

MULTIPURPOSE APPLICATION
http://www.access.gpo.gov/bis/ear/pdf/forms.pdf

B	U.S. DEPARTMENT OF COMMERCE Bureau of Industry and Security	DATE RECEIVED X

FORM BIS-748P
FORM APPROVED: OMB NO. 0694-0088, 0694-0089

MULTIPURPOSE APPLICATION

(Leave Blank)

Information furnished herewith is subject to the provisions of Section 12(c) of the Export Administration Act of 1979, as amended, 50 U.S.C. app. 2411(c), and its unauthorized disclosure is prohibited by law.

1. CONTACT PERSON
2. TELEPHONE
3. FACSIMILE

APPLICATION CONTROL NUMBER
This is NOT an export license number.

Z 306801

4. DATE OF APPLICATION

5. TYPE OF APPLICATION
- EXPORT
- REEXPORT
- CLASSIFICATION REQUEST
- SPECIAL COMPREHENSIVE LICENSE
- OTHER

6. DOCUMENTS SUBMITTED WITH APPLICATION
- BIS-748P-A
- BIS-748P-B
- BIS-711
- IMPORT/END-USER CERTIFICATE
- TECH. SPECS.
- NUCLEAR CERTIFICATION
- LETTER OF EXPLANATION
- FOREIGN AVAILABILITY
- OTHER

7. DOCUMENTS ON FILE WITH APPLICANT
- BIS-711
- LETTER OF ASSURANCE
- IMPORT/END-USER CERTIFICATE
- OTHER

8. SPECIAL COMPREHENSIVE LICENSE
- BIS-752 OR BIS-752-A
- INTERNAL CONTROL PROGRAM
- COMPREHENSIVE NARRATIVE
- CERTIFICATIONS
- OTHER

9. SPECIAL PURPOSE
10. RESUBMISSION APPLICATION CONTROL NUMBER
11. REPLACEMENT LICENSE NUMBER
12. FOR ITEM(S) PREVIOUSLY EXPORTED, PROVIDE LICENSE EXCEPTION SYMBOL OR LICENSE NUMBER
13. IMPORT/END-USER CERTIFICATE COUNTRY: NUMBER:

14. APPLICANT / 15. OTHER PARTY AUTHORIZED TO RECEIVE LICENSE
16. PURCHASER / 17. INTERMEDIATE CONSIGNEE
18. ULTIMATE CONSIGNEE / 19. END-USER
20. ORIGINAL ULTIMATE CONSIGNEE / 21. SPECIFIC END-USE
22. (a) ECCN (b) CTP (c) MODEL NUMBER (d) CCATS NUMBER
23. TOTAL APPLICATION DOLLAR VALUE
(e) QUANTITY (f) UNITS (g) UNIT PRICE (h) TOTAL PRICE (i) MANUFACTURER
(j) TECHNICAL DESCRIPTION
24. ADDITIONAL INFORMATION

25. SIGNATURE (of person authorized to execute this application) NAME OF SIGNER TITLE OF SIGNER

X X ORIGINAL B

USCOMM-DC 96-24024

Appendix L

SAMPLE TAA/MLA TRANSMITTAL LETTER

May 7, 20xx
Applicant Code: M-0000
USML Categories: XI c and XI d

Armageddon Aerospace Corporation
1234 South Rd.
Anywhere, Va. 98765

Mr. Kevin Maloney
Director, Office of Defense Trade Controls Licensing
2401 E Street N.W., Suite 1200 (SA-1)
Washington, D.C. 20522-0112

Subject: Proposed Technical Assistance Agreement (or Manufacturing License Agreement) for the support (or manufacture) of the How to Write Agreements Processor

References: TA 0000-08; DSP-5 000000000

Dear Mr. Maloney

Submitted herewith are an original and seven collated copies of this submission package which includes this letter, a certification letter and the proposed Technical Assistance Agreement for the transfer of certain technical information, hardware (if applicable) and services necessary for the integration, troubleshooting, and maintenance of the How to Write Agreements Processor.

BACKGROUND

Provide a brief description on the purpose of the agreement and how it will be executed by the parties to include scope, role of parties, review of defense articles and services to be transferred.

REQUIRED INFORMATION

In accordance with §124.12, the following information is provided:

(a)(1) The DDTC applicant code is M-0000.

(a)(2) The parties to this agreement are as follows:

The foreign licensee(s)

XXX Technologies
Full Address (no P.O. Box)
Country

AAAA Systems Incorporated

Full Address (no P.O. Box)
Country

U.S. Signatories

U.S. Agreement Writers Guild

Full Address (no P.O. Box)

The scope of this agreement entails (Applicant) performing defense services (or manufacturing know-how if an MLA) or disclosing technical data or providing defense articles (applicant should provide a one-line description) to the licensee for the (briefly identify task to be performed) of (commodity or program) for end-use by (identify end-use and end-user, if applicable).

This agreement is valid until March 31, 20xx.

(a)(3) Identify relevant U.S. Government contracts under which equipment or technical data was generated, improved or developed and supplied to the U.S. Government (to include any relationship to any Foreign Military Sales (FMS) case), and whether the equipment or technical data was derived from any bid or other proposal to the U.S. Government. If none, so state and identify cognizant U.S. military service.

(a)(4) The highest U.S. military security classification of the equipment or technical data to be transferred under the terms of this agreement is (Unclassified, Confidential, Secret or Top Secret). (If foreign classified equipment or technical data is to be transferred, state as such).

(a)(5) State whether any patent requests which disclose any of the subject matter of the equipment or related technical data covered by an invention secrecy order issued by the U.S. Patent and Trademark Office are on file concerning this agreement. If so, the patents must be listed herein.

(a)(6) The estimated value of this agreement is as follows:

Technical Data and Defense Services	$600,000

Hardware
    Permanent Export by DSP-5 or DSP-85
    Temporary Export by DSP-73 or DSP-85
    Temporary Import by DSP-61 or DSP-85
Total Licensed Hardware
	
	$500,000
	$200,000
	$100,000
	$800,000

Hardware Manufactured Abroad (MLA only)	$N/A
AGREEMENT TOTAL VALUE	$1,400,000

If the value of the agreement is $500,000 or greater and for end-use by the armed forces of a foreign government or an international organization, an additional statement must be made regarding the payment of political contributions, fees or commissions, pursuant to Part 130. If none have been paid, a statement must be provided to this effect. If payments have been made, please provide a separate statement signed by the empowered official.

This agreement does not require Congressional Notification pursuant to §123.15 or §124.11. (*If yes, an additional statement indicating whether an offset agreement is proposed to be entered into in connection with the agreement and a description of any such offset agreement must be included*).

(a)(7) Applicant must provide a statement indicating whether any foreign military sales credits or loan guarantees are or will be involved in financing the agreement.

(a)(8) The agreement must describe any classified information involved (U.S. or foreign) and identify, from DoD form DD 254, the address and telephone number of the U.S. Government office that classified the information and the classification source (i.e., document). If no classified information is involved, so state, but do not omit.

(a)(9) For agreements that may require the export of classified information, the Defense

Security Service cognizant security offices that have responsibility for the facilities of the U.S. parties to the agreement shall be identified. The facility security clearance codes of the U.S. parties shall also be provided. If no classified information is involved, so state, but do not omit.

(a)(10) This agreement does (or does not) request retransfer of defense articles and defense services pursuant to §124.16."

Pursuant to §124.8(5), this agreement does (or does not) request access for dual/third country national employees as addressed in Article I(4) of the proposed agreement.

REQUIRED STATEMENTS

(b)(1) If the agreement is approved by the Department of State, such approval will not be construed by the applicant as passing on the legality of the agreement from the standpoint of antitrust laws or other applicable statutes, nor will the applicant construe the Department's approval as constituting either approval or disapproval of any of the business terms or conditions between the parties to the agreement.

(b)(2) The applicant will not permit the proposed agreement to enter into force until it has been approved by the Department of State.

(b)(3) The applicant will furnish the Department of State with one copy of the signed agreement (or amendment) within 30 days from the date that the agreement is concluded and will inform the Department of its termination not less than 30 days prior to the expiration and provide information on the continuation of any foreign rights or the flow of technical data to the foreign party. If a decision is made not to conclude the proposed agreement, the applicant will so inform the Department within 60 days.

(b)(4) If this agreement grants any rights to sub-license, it will be amended to require that all sub-licensing arrangements incorporate all the provisions of the basic agreement that refer to the U.S. Government and the Department of State (i.e., §124.8 and 124.9).

Sub-licensing rights **ARE** granted to the licensee(s) under this agreement as specified in Article I.4(b) of the proposed agreement. or Sub-licensing rights **ARE NOT** granted to the licensee(s) under this agreement as specified in Article I.4(b) of the proposed agreement.

To facilitate U.S. Government consideration of this request, the following information is provided:

Defense articles intended for export in furtherance of this agreement will be shipped via separate license (e.g., DSP-5. DSP-73, etc.).

This agreement relates to the following U.S. Munitions List category(ies): XIc and XId (list applicable USML category and article from §121). These category(ies) are not or are designated as Significant Military Equipment (SME). *For multiple categories, state which are designated SME. If hardware will be exported, then identify whether it/they is/are SME.*

If the agreement involves the transfer of classified technical data or technical data for the manufacture of SME abroad, state whether a Non-transfer and Use Certificate (Form DSP-83), is/is not attached in accordance with §124.10. If the agreement involves the transfer of SME or classified defense articles, state that a DSP-83 will be submitted as part of the DSP-5 or DSP-85 license request.

This agreement does not require Congressional Notification. If yes, make a statement acknowledging that the agreement will be notified and reference an executive summary a signed contract between the applicant and the foreign licensee, and a description of any direct or indirect offsets associated with the agreement.

Prior Approval or Prior Notification is not required.

If you require additional information, please contact (list license point of contact) at telephone number (area code and number), e-mail name@company.com. *If a law firm or consulting firm is authorized to do business on the applicant's behalf, state as such.*

Sincerely,

_____
(Signature block)

Attachments:
Proposed Agreement
Certification Letter, per §126.13 (*This language may be included in transmittal letter if signed by empowered official.*)
Form DSP-83 (*if applicable*)

Appendix M

Sample TAA/MLA

This agreement is entered into between (*company name*)_____, an entity incorporated in the State of (*state*) _____ with offices at (*company address*) _____ and (*foreign company name(s)*) _____ whose office(s) is/are situated at (*foreign company address(es)*) _____ and is effective upon the date of signature of the last party to sign the agreement. (*If the agreement has a large number of parties involved, then list in bullet format for ease of review.*)

WHEREAS, (*applicant name*) _____ (*Describe the program for which you are providing technical assistance or manufacturing for*) _____ (*and the type of assistance you will provide*) _____ _____.

WHEREAS, (*foreign or other U.S. company name*) _____ (*describe the company's role in the TAA or MLA – have a separate paragraph for each foreign company*) _____ _____ _____.

NOW THEREFORE, the parties desire to enter into the Technical Assistance (*or Manufacturing Licensing*) Agreement as follows:

    1. This Technical Assistance (*or Manufacturing Licensing*) Agreement is intended to (*Provide concise summary of program to be done under the agreement. This summary can be drawn from the Statement of Work. The Statement of Work can be a separate document attached to the TAA or MLA and incorporated by reference within the agreement.*)

    2. It is understood that this Technical Assistance (*or Manufacturing Licensing*) Agreement is entered into as required under U.S. Government Regulations and as such, it is an independent agreement between the parties, the terms of which will prevail, notwithstanding any conflict or inconsistency that may be contained in other arrangements between the parties on the subject matter.

    3. The parties agree to comply with all applicable sections of the International Traffic in Arms Regulations (*ITAR*) of the U.S. Department of State and that more particularly in accordance with such regulations the following conditions apply to this agreement:

I. §124.7

    (1) Describe the defense article to be manufactured and all defense articles to be exported in furtherance or support of this agreement. Describe defense articles by military nomenclature, contract number, Federal Stock Number, name plate data, or other specific information. If no hardware is being manufactured or exported, then state so but do not leave blank. An attachment may be used to list hardware, but must reference such attachments under this article.

Note: Only defense articles listed in the agreement or on an addendum sheet and referenced here will be eligible for export in furtherance of the agreement.

(2) Describe the assistance and technical data, to include any design and manufacturing know-how involved. The applicant may address the assistance and technical data in a separate attachment to the request but must reference the attachment under this article.

(3) This agreement is valid through (*month, day, year*).

(4) Territory.

a. The transfer of technical data, defense articles, and defense services is authorized between the United States and (*list countries of foreign licensees*) for end-use by the government of (*list end-users*).

- For MLAs, specifically identify each country of the proposed sales territory

- If marketing is requested, specifically identify each country of the proposed marketing territories

b. Sub-licensing rights are granted to the foreign licensees (*or list the specific foreign licensee*). Sub-licensees are identified in Attachment _____. (*If a small number of sub-licensees, they can be addressed here as part of the paragraph; if more than 15, provide an electronic copy per Section 3.2.b of these Guidelines*)

Sub-licensees are required to execute a Non-Disclosure Agreement (*NDA*) prior to provision of, or access to the defense articles, technical data or defense services. The executed NDA, referencing the DTC Case number and incorporating all the provisions of the Agreement that refer to the United States Government and the Department of State (i.e., §124.8) will be maintained on file by the applicant for five years from the expiration of the agreement.

- If Sub-licensing and Retransfer is not requested, the applicant must specifically state that sub-licensing/retransfer is not authorized.

c. Dual/Third Country National Employees are not authorized (or) are authorized as follows:

(1) Pursuant to §124.8(5), this agreement authorizes access to defense articles and/or retransfer of technical data/defense services to individuals who are dual/third country national employees of the foreign licensees (*and its approved sub-licensees – if applicable*). The exclusive nationalities authorized are (*list all foreign nationalities of the employees who are not eligible for application of §124.16*). Prior to any access or retransfer, the employee must execute a Non-Disclosure Agreement (NDA) referencing this DTC case number. The applicant must maintain copies of the executed NDAs for five years from the expiration of the agreement.

(2) Pursuant to §124.16, this agreement authorizes access to unclassified defense articles and/or retransfer of technical data/defense services to individuals who are dual/third country national employees of the foreign licensees (*and its approved sub-licensees – if applicable*). The exclusive nationalities authorized are limited to NATO, European Union, Australia, Japan, New Zealand, and Switzerland. All access and/or retransfers must take place completely within the physical territories of these countries or the United States.

NOTE: If requesting dual/third country national employees for access to classified defense articles and/or retransfer of technical data/defense services who otherwise qualify for access pursuant to §124.16, the applicant must specifically identify those

exclusive nationalities under the §124.8(5) clause, and NDAs must be executed for these employees.

 d. The U.S. applicant (or U.S. Signatories) currently employs dual/third country nationals of the following counties who will participate in this program:

II. §124.8 *The following statements must be included verbatim as written in the ITAR.*

(1) This agreement shall not enter into force, and shall not be amended or extended without the prior written approval of the Department of State of the U.S. Government.

(2) This agreement is subject to all United States laws and regulations relating to exports and to all administrative acts of the U.S. Government pursuant to such laws and regulations.

(3) The parties to this agreement agree that the obligations contained in this agreement shall not affect the performance of any obligations created by prior contracts or subcontracts which the parties may have individually or collectively with the U.S. Government.

(4) No liability will be incurred by or attributed to the U.S. Government in connection with any possible infringement of privately owned patent or proprietary rights, either domestic or foreign, by reason of the U.S. Government's approval of this agreement.

(5) The technical data or defense service exported from the United States in furtherance of this agreement and any defense article which may be produced or manufactured from such technical data or defense service may not be transferred to a person in a third country or to a national of a third country except as specifically authorized in this agreement unless the prior written approval of the Department of State has been obtained.

(6) All provisions in this agreement which refer to the United States Government and the Department of State will remain binding on the parties after the termination of the agreement.

III. §124.9(a) *All Manufacturing Licensing Agreements must include the clauses verbatim as required by §124.9(a).*

(1) No export, sale, transfer or other disposition of the licensed article is authorized to any country outside the territory wnerein manufacture or sale is herein licensed without the prior written approval of the U.S. Government unless otherwise exempted by the U.S. Government. Sales or other transfers of the licensed article shall be limited to governments of countries wherein manufacture or sale is hereby licensed and to private entities seeking to procure the licensed article pursuant to a contract with any such government unless the prior written approval of the U.S. Government is obtained.

(2) It is agreed that sales by licensee or its sub-licensees under contract made through the U.S. Government will not include either charges for patent rights in which the U.S. Government holds a royalty-fee license, or charges for data which the U.S. Government has a right to use and disclose to others, which are in the public domain, or which the U.S. Government has acquired

or is entitled to acquire without restrictions upon their use and disclosure to others.

(3) If the U.S. Government is obligated or becomes obligated to pay to the licensor royalties, fees, or other charges for the use of technical data or patents which are involved in the manufacture, use, or sale of any licensed article, any royalties, fees or other charges in connection with purchases of such licensed article from licensee or its sub-licensees with funds derived through the U.S. Government may not exceed the total amount the U.S. Government would have been obligated to pay the licensor directly.

(4) If the U.S. Government has made financial or other contributions to the design and development of any licensed article, any charges for technical assistance or know-how relating to the item in connection with purchases of such articles from licensee or sub-licensees with funds derived through the U.S. Government must be proportionately reduced to reflect the U.S. Government contributions, and subject to the provisions of paragraphs (a)(2) and (3) of this section (be sure you properly reference the paragraph numbering system used in the agreement and not just repeat the ITAR numbering), no other royalties, or fees or other charges may be assessed against U.S. Government funded purchases of such articles. However, charges may be made for reasonable reproduction, handling, mailing, or similar administrative costs incident to the furnishing of such data."

(5) The parties to this agreement agree that an annual report of sales or other transfer pursuant to this agreement of the licensed articles, by quantity, type, U.S. dollar value, and purchaser or recipient, shall be provided by (applicant or licensee) to the Department of State." This clause must specify which party is obligated to provide the annual report. Such reports may be submitted either directly by the licensee or indirectly through the licensor, and may cover calendar or fiscal years. Reports shall be deemed proprietary information by the Department of State and will not be disclosed to unauthorized persons. See §126.10(b) of this subchapter.

(6) (Licensee) agrees to incorporate the following statement as an integral provision of a contract, invoice, or other appropriate document whenever the licensed articles are sold or otherwise transferred:

These commodities are authorized for export by the U.S. Government only to (state the country of ultimate destination or approved sales territory). They may not be resold, diverted, transferred, transshipped, or otherwise be disposed of in any other country, either in their original form or after being incorporated through an intermediate process into other end-items, without the prior written approval of the U.S. Department of State.

§124.9(b). *Additionally, MLA's for the production of SME must include the clauses verbatim required by*

(1) A completed Non-transfer and Use Certificate (DSP-83) must be executed by the foreign end-user and submitted to the Department of State of the United States before any transfer may take place. Note: No substitute may be made for a DSP-83 (e.g., end user's certificate or a DSP-83 like document modified by the foreign party).

(2) The prior written approval of the U.S. Government must be obtained

before entering into a commitment for the transfer of the licensed article by sale or otherwise to any person or government outside of the approved sales territory.

IN WITNESS WHEREOF, the parties hereto have caused this agreement to be executed effective as of the day and year of the last signature of this agreement (or) upon approval of the Department of State (if a signed agreement was submitted and no modifications are directed by proviso).

_____   _____

(Signature block for U.S. person)   *(Signature block for foreign person)*

Appendix N

VENDOR PRODUCT EXPORT QUESTIONNAIRE

Note: This form must be completed by a person with export control responsibility in order to comply with applicable export control regulations.

Supplier Name: _____

Address: _____

Telephone: _____

Email: _____

Manufacturer (if different from suppler):

Address: _____

Telephone: _____

Email: _____

IS the product under the USML, if YES, Please provide the following information:

Part #	Product Description	Mfg	USML Category	SME

If multiple line items, please attach as a supplement

Are you registered with the Department of State: _____ YES   _____ NO

If YES, under what company name do you hold your registration: _____

If NO, please provide the following information:

Part #	Product Description	Mfg	ECCN

If multiple line items, please attach as a supplement

Person providing the above information:

Signature: _____

Name: _____

Title: _____

Company: _____

Location: _____

Telephone: _____

Email: _____

Date: _____

Resources

International Traffic and Arms Regulations
http://www.fas.org/spp/starwars/offdocs/itar/p121.htm#C-VIII

U.S. Census Bureau, Foreign Trade Division
http://www.census.gov/trade

U.S. Export Assistance Center
http://www.export.gov

U.S. Customs and Border Protection
http://www.cbp.gov

Directorate of Defense Trade Controls
http://www.pmddtc.state.gov

Export Administration Regulations
http://www.access.gpo.gov/bis/ear/ear_data.html

Office of Foreign Assets
http://www.treas.gov/offices/enforcement/ofac/

Schedule B online
http://www.census.gov/foreign-trade/schedules/b/#browse

International Trade Administration
http://trade.gov/index.asp

U.S. Bureau of Industry and Security
http://www.bis.doc.gov/